KT-582-468

Thomas Cook

CITYSPOTS
MONTE CARLO

Paul Medbourne

Written by Paul Medbourne
Original photography and research by Ethel Davies
Updated by Nancy Cooper

Published by Thomas Cook Publishing
A division of Thomas Cook Tour Operations Limited
Company registration No: 1450464 England
The Thomas Cook Business Park, 9 Coningsby Road
Peterborough PE3 8SB, United Kingdom
Email: sales@thomascook.com, Tel: +44 (0)1733 416477
www.thomascookpublishing.com

Produced by The Content Works Ltd
Aston Court, Kingsmead Business Park, Frederick Place
High Wycombe, Bucks HP11 1LA
www.thecontentworks.com

Series design based on an original concept by Studio 183 Limited

ISBN: 978-1-84157-872-9

First edition © 2006 Thomas Cook Publishing
This second edition © 2008 Thomas Cook Publishing
Text © Thomas Cook Publishing
Maps © Thomas Cook Publishing/PCGraphics (UK) Limited
Transport map © Communicarta Limited

Series Editor: Kelly Anne Pipes
Production/DTP: Steven Collins

Printed and bound in Spain by GraphyCems

Cover photography (Monte Carlo Casino) © Photoshot/World Pictures

CONTENTS

SYMBOLS KEY

The following symbols are used throughout this book:

ⓐ address ⓣ telephone ⓕ fax ⓦ website address ⓔ email
ⓛ opening times ⓝ public transport connections ⓘ important

The following symbols are used on the maps:

🄸 information office		▣	points of interest
✈ airport		◯	city
✚ hospital		◯	large town
🛡 police station		○	small town
🚉 railway station		═	motorway
✝ cathedral		━	main road
❶ numbers denote		—	minor road
featured cafés & restaurants		—	railway

Hotels and restaurants are graded by approximate price as follows:
£ budget price ££ mid-range price £££ expensive

Abbreviations used in addresses:
av. avenue
blvd boulevard
espl. esplanade
pl. place (square)
prom. promenade
sq. square

◐ *Superyachts adorn the harbour*

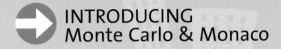

Introduction

Perched precipitously between the Mediterranean and the mountains of the Alpes Maritimes, Monaco is the second-smallest independent state on earth (after the Vatican City), with a surface area of just 2 sq km (less than 1 sq mile) – yet it is known the world over. The name never fails to conjure up associations of millionaires and tax havens, celebrities and fashion, luxury yachts, Grand Prix racing and, of course, the world's most famous casino in Monte Carlo.

Budgeteers will be pleased to hear that, despite all the glitz, Monaco has plenty of sights and attractions to offer non-millionaires – not to mention a superb climate and a handy proximity to Italy and the Côte d'Azur. Visually, it is stunning: every park is a jewel of manicured perfection, their flowers lovingly tended by the veritable army of gardeners that Monaco employs. Its architecture is remarkably bold: Monaco has a reputation for experimenting with brave new styles, a quality that prompted a world architectural expert to comment that 'every great architectural success and mistake made in the past century is represented in Monaco'.

The Principality of Monaco, itself barely the size of a small village, is divided into several distinct mini-towns, of which Monte Carlo is the best known. The official language is French but in practice Monaco is trilingual in French, English and Italian. The Monégasque people (as the locals are known) over the centuries found themselves propelled onto a global stage by the visions of their enterprising monarchs, and now it is estimated that native Monégasques make up only 7,000 of the 35,000 population.

Since the incredibly brazen capture of Monaco by the first Grimaldi (see page 14), little has changed in the ambitious spirit of the royal family. Monaco's face is constantly changing. In recent years, it has seen the arrival of the Grimaldi Forum, a huge and mostly underground conference and leisure centre; the Monte Carlo Bay Hotel, the largest and most ambitious in Monaco's history; the Digue, a floating pier; and Fontvieille, an entire district built on land reclaimed from the sea. Monaco showcases a steady stream of exciting events and exhibitions, and prides itself on championing new creative talent. Monaco has the money, the looks and the fame, but for many its ambitious and innovative spirit is its true wealth.

🔺 *Larvotto beach was created from rock from Monaco's tunnels*

When to go

The emergence of no-frills airlines has made Monaco much more accessible for short breaks from Britain. However, the seasonal fare variations can be staggering: a week's return trip on a low-cost airline from a London airport in July will cost around 30 per cent less than the same journey in August, and early spring can cost a tenth of peak summer. It pays to investigate thoroughly before choosing dates.

Seasonality affects accommodation prices, too. The high season is late July–late August. In the shoulder season, from early April to mid-July and September, rates can be 30–50 per cent lower; if you fancy a late autumn, winter or early spring break you may find hotels offering a further reduction of 10–20 per cent on the mid-season prices. Special accommodation packages in these months offer particularly good value.

SEASONS & CLIMATE

The earliest tourists on the Riviera, mainly wealthy British, came in the 18th and 19th centuries in search of winter warmth. Monaco averages 300 days of sunshine per year, and in winter the daytime temperature stays in the range 8–14°C (48–58°F), with sunny days and cool nights. Spring brings the strong wind of Le Mistral but slightly warmer days, and in summer the temperatures can reach 27°C (80°F), though mitigated by sea breezes, especially in the evening. From the weather point of view September and October are definitely the best months in which to visit – temperatures are a comfortable 15–21°C (60–70°F) and it's still possible to get a tan in October.

ANNUAL EVENTS

For a comprehensive calendar of what's on in the year ahead, check out the tourist authority website Ⓦ www.visitmonaco.com

Motor events

The Automobile Club de Monaco organises two world-famous motor events in the Principality's year. The Monaco Grand Prix always coincides with the public holiday at Ascension in May, and has taken place 65 times since its inauguration in 1929; for more information, see pages 12–13.

Its older cousin, and scarcely less famous, is the Monte Carlo Rally, held in January. The authorities in pre-World War I Monaco, concerned by the dip in tourism and casino revenues caused by the revival of the Carnival in rival Nice, were determined to find an event that would bring the punters back to Monte Carlo and also demonstrate how delightful the climate was in January. Participants were invited to motor to Monte Carlo from cities all over Europe to take part in the inaugural rally in 1911. They still do, though the number of entrants is now limited to 60 and, as the event forms parts of the FIA World Championship, it's a serious competition. Drivers set off from Monte Carlo in each of three legs, on three consecutive days, along circular courses that run well over 100 km (60 miles) across the terrain of the surrounding mountains back to Monte Carlo. 🕐 21–27 Jan 2008; 19–25 Jan 2009 Ⓦ www.acm.mc

Cultural events and performances

Monaco prides itself on having the best of everything. Its music concerts, whether classical, jazz or pop, always showcase the current top global performers. Its ballet, opera and circus performances are world-class and if any play is proving a hit in Paris, you can bet that Monaco will be busy working behind the scenes to bring the show to Monaco.

The tourist office website will keep you up to date (Ⓦ www.monaco-tourisme.com). You can also pick up the monthly booklet *Bienvenue* (see page 153) for information on coming events.

Festivals

The Monégasques love traditional festivals, chief of which are:

January

St Dévote's Day Monaco celebrates its patron saint St Dévote on 27 January, with a public ceremony presided over by Prince Albert at the St Dévote church on the Port Hercule. This is followed by a symbolic burning of a boat. Local children then scour its burnt-out wreckage for nails, said to bring luck for the coming year.

June

Feast of St John the Baptist The evening of 23 June, the eve of the saint's day, sees folk groups from all over the Mediterranean gather to perform traditional music and dance alongside Monaco's own ensemble, the Palladienne, in the Palace Square. The Prince attends a special service in the Palace chapel and then two liveried footmen emerge in the square to light a bonfire. The next day a procession, accompanied by folk groups, forms in place des Moulins in Monte Carlo and marches to the parish church, St-Charles. After a service the crowd returns to the place des Moulins and dances the rest of the day and night away in a great open-air ball.

July

Sciaratù The tradition of having a good time just before the rigours of Lent is as old in Monaco as in nearby Nice, but while Nice's Carnival has become one of the Riviera's major events, in Monaco the event lapsed until about 30 years ago, when it was revived under the local dialect name *Sciaratù* and moved to the summer. Much like the Nice Carnival, it is marked by processions, dummy heads, confetti battles and open-air dancing.

August
Festival of St-Romain A chapel was built in the 16th century to this martyred Roman legionary in the hamlet of Les Moulins, but the festivities now take place every 9 August in the St Martin Gardens of Monaco-Ville, with open-air dancing and a lot of refreshments.

November
Monégasque National Holiday This holiday is celebrated on 19 November, the feast of St Rainier. The daytime is marked by a special mass, after which the reigning Prince distributes honours and decorations. Night-time sees a gala evening at the Opéra and a firework display over the harbour.

PUBLIC HOLIDAYS
Public transport runs to Sunday schedules, and banks, post offices and public buildings are closed on these days. Many shops (but not generally restaurants) will also be closed.
New Year's Day 1 Jan
St Dévote's Day 27 Jan
Easter Monday 24 Mar 2008, 13 Apr 2009
Labour Day 1 May
Ascension Day 1 May 2008, 21 May 2009
Whit Monday 12 May 2008, 1 June 2009
Corpus Christi 22 May 2008, 11 June 2009
Assumption of the Blessed Virgin Mary 15 Aug
All Saints' Day 1 Nov
National Day 19 Nov
Christmas Day 25 Dec

The Monaco Grand Prix

Few events in the Formula 1 Grand Prix season have quite the same excitement as the Monaco Grand Prix: this is the only F1 race that is regularly raced around the streets of a city, and is one of the season's most difficult courses. Millions who have never visited Monaco are familiar with the layout of the city centre through broadcasts of this historic race.

In 1925, the Monaco Cycling Club decided to rename itself the Automobile Club de Monaco, and applied to become a member of the International Association of Recognised Automobile Clubs; it was turned down on the grounds that Monaco organised no motor sport events on its own territory. Stung to the quick, the Monégasques set about removing all the obstacles, physical and organisational, to holding a race through their streets. On 14 April 1929, Prince Pierre inaugurated the 1st Monaco Grand Prix with a lap of honour in a Torpedo Voisin. The 16-car race that followed was won by a Bugatti driven by Williams, an Englishman who had arrived too late to take part in the official trial sessions. The average speed over the 100 laps was just 80 kph (50 mph)!

Today, the course is much the same as the original one, though modifications take place from time to time (notably, in 1976, the addition of the famous Rascasse hairpin bend); its 3.3 km (2 miles) are now raced over 78 laps by around 20 cars. The Monaco Grand Prix takes place each year in late May, the programme extending from Thursday to Sunday, the race day. Normal traffic is barred from the course from 06.00/07.00 to 19.00 Thur–Sat, Thursday being the day for practice runs and Saturday for the F1 qualifying trials. Final qualifying trials take place on the Sunday morning, and at 14.00 on the Sunday the race begins.

Tickets for seats with a view of the race cost from €32 to €46, available from official booths on the day or in advance from the Automobile Club de Monaco. Some restaurants offer lunch menus for tables on their terraces overlooking the circuit. Residents overlooking the course make a small fortune renting out their balconies. Hotel rooms during the race period are very difficult to find, as so many are block-booked annually; better to stay in Menton or even Nice and travel in during this event.

The next dates are: 22–25 May 2008, 21–24 May 2009.

Automobile Club de Monaco ⓐ 23 blvd Albert 1er, 98012 Monaco
ⓣ 93 15 26 00 ⓕ 93 25 80 08 ⓦ www.acm.mc

▲ *Monaco can claim to have the most luxurious trackside seats of any F1 event*

History

Unlike many sovereign states, Monaco can trace its beginnings very precisely to the date of 8 January 1297. Up till then this area of the Italian coast had been a battleground between the two major factions of medieval Italy, the Guelphs (supporters of the Pope) and the Ghibellines (the league of cities and families backing the Holy Roman Emperors, who sought to establish their rule across the entire Italian peninsula in the face of Papal opposition). The Ghibellines had built a castle in 1215 on the site of what is now Monaco's palace, but on that fateful night in 1297, François Grimaldi, a Guelph from Genoa, tricked his way in by disguising his followers as monks, and seized the fortress. François and his successors established themselves as rulers of this strategically important rock and its port, later extending their domain by acquiring nearby Roquebrune and Menton.

By 1489 the two major powers in the area, France and Savoy, were ready to formally acknowledge Monaco's independence. In 1612 the reigning Grimaldi, Honoré II, gave himself the title of Prince of Monaco, and the Principality came into being; he later signed a treaty which effectively tied his country's foreign policy to that of France for good, while reaffirming Monaco's sovereignty, and this has been the status quo ever since. The only interruption to this relationship came with the French Revolution, when the Grimaldis were temporarily dispossessed, but normality was restored in 1814 with the overthrow of Napoleon.

The next big change, which established the character of modern Monaco, came in 1861, when Charles III, unable to prevent the transfer of Roquebrune and Menton to France, realised he needed new sources of revenue. His answer was to found the Casino on the Plateau des Spélugues, renamed Monte Carlo (Charles' Hill), in 1866. With the advent of the railway, bringing wealthy gamblers and tourists from all over Europe, the Principality's fortunes took a steady upswing; Charles' second master-stroke was to exempt residents from most taxes, ensuring the stream of tax exiles from which Monaco has benefited ever since.

The early 20th century saw the reign of the enlightened Albert I, who sponsored the Musée Océanographique (Oceanographic Institute), scientific expeditions to South America and many other technological advances. In 1949 Prince Rainier III came to the throne and caught the world's attention by his story-book marriage to film star Grace Kelly; Princess Grace's death following a motor accident in 1982 was a tragedy shared by the whole world. Although the behaviour of some of the princely family often attracted unwelcome publicity, Rainier himself remained popular until the end of his long reign, dying in 2005 to be succeeded by his son Albert II, the current Prince. Albert, though still unmarried, has a child; the last Prince in this situation was his great-grandfather Louis II, who formally adopted his own illegitimate daughter in order to continue the princely succession legally. Prince Albert II is already acquiring a reputation for encouraging entrepreneurial spirit and environmental responsibility – both within the principality and around the world.

🔺 *His Serene Highness Albert II*

Lifestyle

When Charles III opened the Casino and its associated hotels in 1866 (see page 14), he ushered in the world's first state that was devoted entirely to pleasure – for visitors, that is. Pleasure then meant gambling, shopping, drinking and fine dining, and the clientele was Europe's elite (give or take a few penniless adventurers and con men). It was quickly denounced in other parts of the world as a hell on earth given over to every kind of vice, and with publicity like that it couldn't fail. Today the visitor profile is more democratic, and there are many more cultural and fun attractions than gambling away your inheritance or what scandalised Victorian commentators called 'acts of gallantry' (roughly anything that involved men and women taking their clothes off).

The other side of the picture is less evident to the casual visitor: the 7,000 or so native Monégasque citizens (less than a quarter of the country's population) are a conservative lot, whose pleasures are more likely to be found in traditional saint's day celebrations (see page 10) or quiet family occasions. Apparently untroubled by political or economic issues (they didn't see the need for a national constitution until 1911, for instance), they get on with their lives in an atmosphere of respectability and devotion to the ruling family. By law they can't even enter the Casino except to work there.

This is not to say that they are unfriendly, inhospitable or intolerant of their visitors; however, they do take pains to preserve Monaco's image as an upmarket playground. The most obvious symptom of this is the public dress code. Though topless bathing is fine on the beach, appearing anywhere else in Monaco bare-chested, barefoot or wearing swimsuits will soon invite the attention of the police. It also pays to defer to some of the formal courtesy that the

Monégasques, like the French, observe. Don't forget to say *bonjour* (hello) to the shopkeeper and *au revoir* (goodbye) when you leave the shop; include a *s'il vous plaît* (please) when you ask for something and a *merci* (thank you) when you receive it. Call the waiter *monsieur* and the waitress *mademoiselle*. Unless you are addressed in English first, it is polite to begin a conversation or request with a local in a few words of your best French, if only to establish that you are a civilised visitor and to acknowledge that you are a guest in someone else's country.

● *Luxury motors are all part of Monte Carlo's glamorous lifestyle*

Culture

Monaco's wealth enables it to put on a programme of events in the arts, theatre, opera, ballet and music that is rivalled by only a few of the world's cities. Add to that one or two internationally acclaimed museums, and it is easy to see why this tiny country attracts so many culture vultures.

Since its creation in 1879, the Opéra de Monte Carlo has gained international fame, playing a key role in promoting the most beautiful voices to the rest of Europe and maintains a reputation for artistic innovation. Historically, composers of the calibre of Bizet, Franck and Massenet chose the Monte Carlo Opera to début their works. Today, it maintains a classical repertoire mixed with more modern newcomers. Performances are held not only in the original Salle Garnier of the Casino (see page 64), but also in newer venues such as the Grimaldi Forum (see page 65) and the Espace Fontvieille (see page 103).

The Monte Carlo Ballet Company started as a dance academy, founded by Princess Grace; restructured in 1985 under choreographer Jean-Christophe Maillot, it is reviving the Principality's formerly strong tradition in ballet, with the aim of bringing Monaco once more up to the highest international level in this field.

The Monte Carlo Philharmonic Orchestra was first established in 1863. Many great conductors of the 20th century, from Arturo Toscanini to Leonard Bernstein and Lorin Maazel, have led the orchestra in concert.

Bookings and programme for performance arts ⓐ Atrium du Casino de Monte Carlo, pl. du Casino ⓣ 98 06 28 28 ⓛ 10.00–17.30 Tues–Sun ⓦ www.monaco-spectacle.com

The most visible evidence of the Grimaldis' commitment to the visual arts is the astonishing Chemins des Sculptures (Sculpture

Trail), which decorates the whole length of Monaco before coming to a grand climax in the Parc Paysager de Fontvieille (Fontvieille Park) (see page 103). Monaco has always attracted artists, and today there are many temporary exhibitions of art on themes as diverse as Latin

🔺 *The Monte Carlo Ballet Company*

American sculpture to 'Dali at Monte Carlo'. For a more permanent exhibition, the Marlborough Gallery (see page 92) is the place to view the output of Monaco's contemporary crop of artists.

Although a number of Monaco's museums are more visitor attractions than cultural centres, at least two are world leaders in the study of their subjects. The Oceanographic Institute (see page 84), founded in the early 20th century by the scientifically minded Prince Albert I, is at the forefront of oceanic research, and its excellent museum should be visited by anyone with even the slightest interest in marine wildlife and conservation. Its botanical equivalent is the Jardin Exotique (Exotic Garden) (see page 90), where the dry-climate plants of the world are grown, studied and propagated; the terraced garden of cacti and other succulents is fascinating at any time of the year. Although the subject may appear trivial in comparison, the collection of dolls and moving figures lovingly assembled by Mme Madeleine Galéa and bequeathed to the Musée National de Monaco (page 66) is a delight. Those with more of a need for speed will find plenty to interest them in Prince Rainier's collection of 20th-century automobiles at the Collection des Voitures Anciennes (Classic Car Exhibition) in Fontvieille (see page 105).

▶ *The place du Casino is the very heart of Monte Carlo*

Shopping

It has to be said that Monaco is not the place for bargains. Not surprisingly, in view of the presence of so many millionaires in its population, every famous designer name has an establishment here, along with a lot of upmarket local specialists. Anyone seeking cheap designer fashions would do better to head for the market at Ventimiglia, though the designer goods there are fakes (see page 131).

If your credit card will stand it, or if you are a relentless window shopper, there are plenty of shops to keep you entertained in Monaco. There are also markets and plenty of hypermarkets and humbler shops, especially in La Condamine and the Fontvieille Centre Commercial, where you can acquire the foodstuffs and goods that attract foreign shoppers to France.

Whatever your shopping needs, high-flying or mundane, you'll find the booklet *Monaco Shopping* invaluable; obtainable from the tourist office, this annual publication lists everything from dry cleaners to antiques emporia, hairdressers to high-class jewellers.

La Condamine is the best area for mainstream shopping. This is where you'll find the main food and flower market and the pedestrianised rue Princesse Caroline shopping centre. Being near the yacht harbour of Port Hercule it also has a host of shops specialising in marine paraphernalia. It's the best place in town to look for genuine regional produce, and has the Principality's main quota of useful everyday shops – small supermarkets, pharmacies and the like. The more upmarket streets of Monte Carlo don't exactly lack butchers and bakers, either, but you may not notice them among the top-name designer outlets, the jewellers and couturiers.

● *Boulevard des Moulins, one of the most fashionable shopping streets*

USEFUL SHOPPING PHRASES

What time do the shops open/close?
A quelle heure ouvrent/ferment les magasins?
Ah kehlur oovr/fehrm leh mahgazhan?

How much is this?
C'est combien?
Cey combyahn?

Can I try this on?
Puis-je essayer ceci?
Pweezh ehssayeh cerssee?

My size is ...
Ma taille (clothes)/ma pointure (shoes) est ...
Mah tie/mah pooahngtewr ay ...

I'll take this one, thank you
Je prends celui-ci/celle-ci merci
Zher prahng serlweesi/sehlsee mehrsee

The Centre Commercial le Métropole, at the hotel of the same name (see page 39) facing the Casino gardens, alone has 80 shops, as well as cafés and restaurants for refreshment. However, the further north you stroll along Monte Carlo's boulevards, the more varied the shops become. Residential Fontvieille has its own, more down-to-earth Centre Commercial, including a Carrefour hypermarket for food and general goods (yet another good place to pick up the contents of a picnic). In the narrow streets of Monaco-Ville, the old town, whatever space is not taken up by bistros and cafés goes to small craftsmen and visitor-oriented gift shops.

🔺 *The Métropole is Monte Carlo's most upmarket shopping centre*

Eating & drinking

There's haute cuisine aplenty in central Monte Carlo, as you would expect, both in the dining rooms of the top hotels and in fashionable cafés and bistros, many of them attached to a major nightlife centre, such as the Casino and the Sporting Club. But even in Monte Carlo, and certainly in nearly every other district of Monaco (with the possible exception of Moneghetti), there's no shortage of more affordable options for lunch and dinner. La Condamine offers perhaps the widest choice of cheap-to-medium eating, both in the port area and just behind it, especially around the place d'Armes and its covered market. In residential Fontvieille most of the dining is on the waterfront, though there are one or two good options close to the park and Princess Grace Rose Garden. Fontvieille has a large shopping complex (the Centre Commercial de Fontvieille) that offers a range of bars, cafés, low-cost brasseries and fast-food outlets. Monaco-Ville's narrow streets are full of cafés and bistros where the accent is often on traditional local cuisine.

PRICE CATEGORIES

The following price guide, used throughout the book, indicates the average price per head for a two- to three-course dinner, excluding drinks. Lunch will usually be a little cheaper in each category.

£ Under €40   ££ €40–70   £££ Over €70

● *The grandest of grand restaurants – the Salle Empire at the Hôtel de Paris*

Restaurant bills are often *service compris* (check for the phrase *sce compris* on your bill) – so unless you have had really good service, or you are dining in one of the very best restaurants, there's no need to tip. At most, you might leave the small change behind after a drink in a café. The major credit cards are accepted everywhere for all but the cheapest meals. By law all restaurants should have a non-smoking area (*espace non-fumeur*).

Strictly vegetarian establishments are thin on the ground, but Mediterranean and especially Italian cuisine, which is popular at all expense levels, on the whole provides plenty of tasty non-meat and non-fish options, and most restaurants of any pretension will have specific vegetarian dishes on the menu.

FOOD SPECIALITIES & PICNICS

Almost every kind of cooking style is available in cosmopolitan Monaco. The most popular flavours, understandably, are Provençal, Italian and general Mediterranean, brought to a refined level in the top-class kitchens; but you don't have to go far to find Chinese, Japanese, Thai, Tex-Mex, North African and other regional cuisines, and even a few English-style pubs and Irish bars.

Underneath this cosmopolitan fare, you can still find some truly Monégasque specialities in bakeries and takeaways all around town. These include *barbajuan*, a small pie filled with rice and squash, *fougasse*, a nut-topped pastry flavoured with orange-flower water and *socca*, a chick-pea pancake that is a favourite street food in the markets. More substantial is *stocafi*, the local take on that favourite Mediterranean combination of salt cod, oil, tomatoes and black olives – at its most authentic in the little bistros of Monaco-Ville.

Even if these local dishes don't whet your appetite, the high quality of bread, fresh produce and *charcuterie* (deli food) in Monaco's markets and small shops, and even in the supermarkets of the shopping centres, should tempt you to take a picnic lunch to the beach or one of Monaco's green spaces.

USEFUL DINING PHRASES

I would like a table for ... people
Je voudrais une table pour ... personnes
Zher voodray ewn tabl poor ... pehrson

Waiter/waitress!
Monsieur/Mademoiselle!
M'sewr/madmwahzel!

May I have the bill, please?
L'addition, s'il vous plaît!
Laddyssyohn, sylvooplay!

Could I have it well-cooked/medium/rare please?
Je le voudrais bien cuit/à point/saignant
Zher ler voodray beeang kwee/ah pwan/saynyang

I am a vegetarian. Does this contain meat?
Je suis végétarien (végétarienne). Est-ce que ce plat contient de la viande?
Zher swee vehzhehtarianhg (vehzhehtarien). Essker ser plah kontyang der lah veeahngd?

Where is the toilet (restroom) please?
Où sont les toilettes, s'il vous plaît?
Oo sawng leh twahlaitt, sylvooplay?

Entertainment & nightlife

There is just so much happening in Monaco, especially in Monte Carlo and especially in the summer months, that the following just scratches the surface. To get a full overview of what's on during your visit, make sure you call at the tourist office for your copy of its invaluable monthly update *Bienvenue* (see page 153) just as soon as you arrive, or to make plans in advance by visiting
ⓦ www.monaco-tourisme.com

CASINOS

Think of Monte Carlo and you'll think of casinos. Even if you don't intend to gamble away the family silver on your trip, there's nothing to stop you paying the relatively modest fee to enter one of the Principality's high-class gaming halls and take in the atmosphere.

Of course, the real high-roller games take place out of the public gaze, but there's still something irresistible about all the raw tension in the upmarket setting of the public tables. (If you're a member of the clergy, you needn't worry about compromising your principles – under Monégasque law they won't let you in anyway.) The lower age limit to enter a casino in Monaco is 21, and you'll need to bring your passport.

Monte Carlo has four grand and fashionable casinos, all owned by the Société des Bains de Mer (SBM), the company that Prince Charles III set up to run his new venture in the 1860s. (The SBM owns nearly every major public venue in Monte Carlo, in fact, including many of its best hotels – and the ruling family of Monaco owns two-thirds of the SBM.) In addition to the Casino, almost next door you'll find the casino of the Café de Paris and the Sun Casino at the Fairmont Monte Carlo (see pages 70–2 for more on these); further

KNOW YOUR ROULETTE
For the uninitiated, French roulette is the kind where everybody crowds round the table, while the English version has a limited number of table seats and the players all bet in chips of their own colour. American roulette gives the bank two chances of taking everyone's money, with a 'o' and a 'oo' on the wheel.

north, past the beach of Larvotto, is Le Sporting (see pages 71–2), where the jet-setters frequent the Salle des Palmiers.

CINEMA

The good news for English-speaking visitors is that both of Monaco's top cinemas often show films in *version originale* (VO), i.e. with their original soundtracks. So if they are showing the latest Hollywood release, you can hear it in English with French subtitles on screen. For details of what's on and screening times, check with *Bienvenue* ❶ 92 68 00 72 or ⓦ www.cinemasporting.com

Cinema d'Eté en plein air Monaco's coolest cinema in every sense, this is the city's open-air summer cinema. Films are shown every evening on the biggest outdoor screen in Europe, on the roof of the big car park at the tip of Monaco-Ville. ⓐ Terrasses du Parking des Pêcheurs ⓛ 25 June–10 Sept ⓝ Bus: 1, 2 to Monaco-Ville

Cinema le Sporting Three indoor screens in the heart of Monte Carlo. ⓐ pl. du Casino ⓛ Three performances weekdays and Sun, four on Sat ⓝ Bus: 1, 2, 6 to Casino

CLUBS, DISCOS & BARS

Monte Carlo is home to Monaco's glitziest bars and nightclubs, while Fontvieille has the more relaxed, family-oriented venues and La Condamine the studenty hangouts. Monaco's reputation for high-class glamour is mostly thanks to Monte Carlo's nightlife and it comes as a pleasant surprise to find that there is a lot more variety in Monaco than its reputation might suggest. The endearingly worn Café Grand Prix (see page 98), for instance, is an enormously popular bar, club and restaurant on the port attracting rock musicians, backpackers and everyone in between. The Stars'N'Bars (see pages 97–8) is a lively sports bar and was a popular haunt of Prince Albert II before he became ruler.

SHOWS & EVENTS

Monaco is good at shows. If you fancy dressing up a bit and enjoying a traditional dinner and cabaret evening, then reserve your table at the Cabaret du Casino or the Salle des Etoiles le Sporting (page 72), both in Monte Carlo. The frequent Gala Evenings at the Salle des Etoiles, some of them in aid of causes such as the Red Cross, are the ultimate in glamour, and there is nothing to stop you dressing up to the nines and going along to enjoy top performers and rock bands while doing some serious celeb spotting. At the other end of the scale, there's a lively programme of outdoor entertainment called **Le Fort Antoine dans la Ville**, which sees concerts, spectacles and comedy performances all summer in the place d'Armes and elsewhere. For information on the current programme, check *Bienvenue* or ❶ 98 98 83 03

▶ *Old-style glamour, complete with showgirls, at the Cabaret du Casino*

Sport & relaxation

BEACHES & WATERSPORTS

Monaco doesn't have the wide beaches of other resort areas. Only one worthy of the name lies in the Principality itself – the public Plage du Larvotto (see page 76) at the far north of Monaco's coast. Further along the avenue Princesse Grace is Monte Carlo Beach, which is actually in France. In fact, most of the best beaches lie just outside Monaco, north and south along the Riviera. On the other hand, Monaco provides top-class swimming facilities: two Olympic pools (Stade Nautique Rainier III and Stade Louis II – see pages 99 and 104), not to mention excellent pools in hotels, at the Thermes Marins and even the municipal pool (ⓐ 7 av. St-Charles). Be advised that while topless sunbathing is tolerated, nude isn't. And change back to day clothes when you leave the beach – swimwear on the streets is a no-no.

OTHER OUTDOOR ACTIVITIES

Monaco offers plenty of healthy ways to see the town – hire a boat, play a round of golf, rent a bicycle, or just walk or jog.

There are many agencies that charter yachts or powerboats – the *Bienvenue* provides a list. You can hire two wheels – cycle or scooter – for the day from: **Auto-Moto-Garage** ⓐ 7 rue de Milo ⓣ 93 50 10 80 **Monte-Carlo Rent** ⓐ quai des Etats-Unis (north side of Port Hercule) ⓣ 99 99 97 79/06 67 33 61 73

Fancy a game of tennis or squash? Try one of these clubs: **Monte-Carlo Country Club** ⓐ av. Princess Grace, St-Roman (just across the border north of Larvotto) ⓣ 00 33 4 93 41 30 15 **Monte-Carlo Squash Racket Club** ⓐ Stade Louis II, av. des Castelans (Fontvieille) ⓣ 92 05 42 22

Tennis Club de Monaco ⓐ 5 Moyenne Corniche, Cap d'Ail (France)
ⓣ 93 30 01 02

The nearest golf club is a 20-minute drive away in the hills behind
Monaco (and so technically in France). The **Monte-Carlo Golf Club**
has an 18-hole course, par 71, as well as practice range. You need a
handicap of 35 (32 at weekends) to play there. ⓐ Mont Agel, La Turbie
ⓣ 00 33 4 92 41 50 70. For serious exercise, Monaco also has two
jogging trails: one is a 2.5 km (1.5 mile) tiered track along the
boulevard du Jardin Exotique in Moneghetti, and a shorter one
along the boulevard du Larvotto.

SPAS & FITNESS

Monaco has a number of upmarket spas, the best of which is the
world-renowned Thermes Marins (see page 77). Spa treatments in
Monaco are fairly traditional but performed to a high standard. The
spas attached to hotels tend to have a juice bar and their own healthy
food menu. The Thermes Marins' restaurant 'L'Hirondelle' is the best
for healthy options and is a great restaurant in its own right.

SPECTATOR SPORTS

A full programme of top-class events starts with the Monte Carlo
Rally, and its companion the Historic Monte Carlo Rally, in January
(see page 9). April sees a Tennis Masters tournament at the Country
Club and the international Show Jumping Championship and, of
course, May brings the Monaco Grand Prix (see pages 12–13).
Swimming takes over the arena in June, followed by the Monaco
Classic Week in September, an international event for classic yachts
and motor boats. November rounds off the year with the Monaco
International Marathon. If soccer is your sport, then go along to
Stade Louis II to watch one of Europe's top clubs, AS Monaco.

Accommodation

Monaco offers over 2,100 hotel beds in categories ranging from the highest luxury, clustered around the Casino area, down to 3- and 2-star establishments in the outlying areas of the Principality, especially La Condamine; the latter include motels and representatives of chains such as Ibis. There are no youth hostels, backpacker hotels or campsites within the borders of the Principality, though; if you're on a really tight budget your best option is to stay at a hostel or campsite in one of the neighbouring French Riviera resorts, for example around Nice, and travel into Monaco, making use of its excellent transport links. This applies equally to hotels: you may find a hotel closer to your requirements and at better rates just outside the Principality, at Menton or along the Nice–Monaco stretch of the Riviera, for instance.

Breakfast is almost always charged extra; upmarket hotels lay on a full buffet, but some others stick to the Continental minimum of coffee, juice and rolls. If your hotel doesn't provide the kind of breakfast you want, take your *petit déjeuner* at a café instead (many of which offer an 'English' or 'American' breakfast).

Unless you have booked an inclusive package, it pays to investigate thoroughly on the web; in addition to hotels' own web pages and

PRICE CATEGORIES

The following ratings indicate average price per double room per night – some rooms may be more or less expensive than the rating suggests.

£ Under €150 ££ €150–300 £££ Over €300 (note: rates in the grandest hotels can be considerably over this level)

the many hotel-finder sites, the tourist office offers listings and instant reservations at ⓦ www.monaco-tourisme.com. Special packages and offers, especially for the quieter seasons, abound. Listed below are a few recommendations, but there are plenty of other good hotels to choose from.

HOTELS

Hôtel de France £ Situated in the La Condamine area, this hotel offers 26 rooms with all the basic facilities and pleasant, if unremarkable, decor. ⓐ 6 rue de la Turbie ⓣ 93 30 24 64 ⓦ www.monte-carlo.mc/france ⓝ Bus: 1, 2, 4, 6 to Place d'Armes

Le Versailles £ A 2-star hotel, situated like most others in its category in La Condamine, the Versailles has just 15 rooms and a large restaurant. ⓐ 4 av. Prince-Pierre ⓣ 93 50 79 34 ⓦ www.monte-carlo.mc/versailles ⓝ Bus: 1, 2, 4, 6 to Place d'Armes

Ambassador-Monaco £–££ Housed in a 19th-century building, the Ambassador has 35 rooms and an Italian restaurant, as well as a private beach for summer guests. ⓐ 10 av. Prince-Pierre ⓣ 97 97 96 96 ⓦ www.ambassadormonaco.com ⓝ Bus: 1, 2, 4, 6 to Place d'Armes

Miramar £–££ Nicely situated close to the harbour, the Miramar has just 11 rooms, all with sea views, and a restaurant and wine/tapas bar. ⓐ 1 av. du Président Kennedy ⓣ 93 30 86 48 ⓦ www.hotel-miramar.mc ⓝ Bus: 1, 2, 6 to Ostende

Tulip Inn Monaco Terminus £–££ A recently renovated, modern establishment close to the railway station and Fontvieille. The 54 rooms have air-conditioning and sound-proofing; 12 of them face the sea.

⬤ *The Tulip Inn is one of several good-value hotels in La Condamine*

There is also a restaurant and a tapas bar. ⓐ 9 av. Prince-Pierre
ⓘ 92 05 63 00 Ⓦ www.terminus.monte-carlo.mc Ⓝ Bus: 1, 2, 4, 6
to Place d'Armes

Columbus Monaco ££ Although it markets itself particularly as a
business/conference venue, this chic 181-room hotel has a lot to offer
leisure tourists who want something stylish at an affordable price.
Situated in Fontvieille, it has views of the sea and also the Princess
Grace Rose Garden, and offers a fitness area and outdoor pool.
ⓐ 23 av. des Papalins ⓘ 92 05 9000 Ⓦ www.columbushotels.com
Ⓝ Bus: 5, 6 to Papalins

Le Méridien Beach Plaza ££–£££ If relaxation is high on your agenda
then this hotel-resort's three swimming pools and private beach

may be just what you're looking for. All of the 338 rooms have a private balcony and most have sea views, and in addition to the year-round rooftop restaurant there's an informal buffet-grill in the summer. ⓐ 22 av. Princesse-Grace ⓣ 93 30 98 80 ⓦ www.lemeridien-montecarlo.com ⓝ Bus: 4, 6 to Larvotto

Hôtel de Paris £££ One of the original deluxe hotels built for the first guests of the Casino, this legendary establishment has a guest book filled with famous names from the last century and a half. Service and accommodation is totally up to date, however. One of its three restaurants is master chef Alain Ducasse's Louis XV (see page 74) in La Salle Empire, an architectural as well as a gastronomic tour de force. ⓐ pl. du Casino ⓣ 98 06 30 00 ⓦ www.montecarloresort.com ⓝ Bus: 1, 2, 6 to Casino

Hôtel Métropole £££ A recent refurbishment has transformed the Métropole into one of Monaco's most romantic hotels. Refitted to resemble the interior of a Venetian palazzo, the new Métropole is sumptuous and houses the newly Michelin-starred Joel Robuchon restaurant. ⓐ 4 av. de la Madone ⓣ 93 15 15 15 ⓦ www.metropole.com ⓝ Bus: 1, 2, 6 to Casino

Monte-Carlo Bay Hotel & Resort £££ The SBM's newest project, the Monte-Carlo Bay Hotel is Monaco's first resort hotel. Built to rival the ambitious resorts springing up in Dubai, it is located next to Jimmy'z nightclub and the Sporting club – and has several new restaurants (of which the Blue Bay is the crowning glory), as well as an incredible multi-level swimming pool. ⓐ av. Princesse Grace ⓣ 98 06 02 00 ⓦ http://montecarlobay.com/ ⓝ Bus: 4, 6 to Larvotto

Monte Carlo Beach Hotel £££ With just 47 rooms, this is one of the smaller luxury hotels in Monaco, a 1930s resort tucked away by the sea on the northern tip of the bay of Monaco, just outside the Principality's borders. It boasts three restaurants and a private beach. ⓐ av. Princess-Grace, St-Roman, 06190 Roquebrune-Cap-Martin ⓣ 98 06 50 00 ⓛ Mar–mid-Nov ⓦ www.montecarloresort.com

SELF-CATERING

For stays of a week or more, especially if travelling as a family, it may well be worth considering renting a villa or an apartment. Again, there is plenty of help on the web, but a very useful resource for apartments just outside Monaco, at Cap d'Ail and Beausoleil, is ⓦ www.monaco-hotel.com (navigate to 'Résidences')

If you are looking for a very central location and expense is not a concern, then the following luxury apartments rent by the week or longer (or purchase on a time-share basis).

Le Castel Residence £££ Located on the hillside overlooking La Condamine and the sea, with views of the Rocher de Monaco. ⓐ 9 av. Corvetto Frères, Monte Carlo ⓣ 97 97 12 97 ⓦ www.lecastel.com

The ultimate in convenience would be to rent your own villa:

Villa La Vigie £££ The villa stands on Pointe de la Vigie, between Monaco, Roquebrune-Cap-Martin and the sea. This imposing three-storey structure, surrounded by a wooded park with Mediterranean trees, enjoys breathtaking panoramic views over the sea. Agency: ⓐ 20 blvd des Moulins, Monte Carlo ⓣ 93 50 30 70 ⓔ info@johntaylormonaco.com

⬛ *The doyenne of Monte Carlo hotels occupies the best position in town*

THE BEST OF MONTE CARLO & MONACO

To get a speedy overview of what Monaco has to offer, one option is a ready-made tour. In addition to the helicopter tours described on page 100, there are two tour options, one cheap, one rather expensive.

Tourist train A quick way of discovering the secrets of the old town is to take the Azur Express, the tourist 'train' that departs from outside the Musée Océanographique for a 30-minute tour of Monaco-Ville. 🛈 92 05 64 38 🕐 Daily

Monte-Carlo Limousine If you have the urge to do things in style, splash out on your own personal guided tour in a limousine with a multilingual chauffeur/guide. 📍 Fairmont Monte Carlo Hotel, 12 av. des Spélugues 🛈 93 50 82 65

TOP 10 SIGHTS & EXPERIENCES

- **Casino de Monte Carlo** You don't have to be a gambler to visit the world-famous institution that is virtually synonymous with Monte Carlo (see page 70).

- **Palais Princier (Prince's Palace)** Tour the state apartments of the Grimaldis and absorb the history of this tiny but independent country (see page 81).

🔻 *Boats and yachts in Monaco's harbour*

- **Dinner for two** It could be the acme of haute cuisine at one of Monte Carlo's grandest hotels or a simple meal at a small restaurant overlooking one of Monaco's two harbours.

- **Princess Grace Rose Garden** Recharge your spiritual batteries in this fragrant haven, tucked away in quiet Fontvieille (see page 103).

- **Spa treatment** Treat yourself to renewal and a sense of well-being from the therapies of the Thermes Marins (see page 77) or one of the other luxurious spas in Monte Carlo.

- **Le Sporting** Put on your glad rags and rub shoulders with the rich and famous at one of this legendary venue's Gala Evenings (see page 71).

- **Oceanographic Museum** A world-class museum of marine life with fascinating aquarium and shark tank (see page 84).

- **Jardin Exotique and Grotte de L'Observatoire (Observatory Cave)** Two contrasting experiences in one place – an internationally acclaimed garden of amazing plants and a deep, stalagmite-filled cave once inhabited by Stone Age man (see page 90).

- **Dance the night away** in glamorous company at clubs such as Jimmy'z (see page 71) or at the Grimaldi Forum (page 65).

- **Watch the Grand Prix** Reserve a trackside table at a restaurant overlooking the course and enjoy the excitement of the race over a leisurely lunch (see page 12).

Suggested itineraries

HALF-DAY: MONACO IN A HURRY

If you're just calling into Monaco on a longer Riviera holiday, or maybe catching some sightseeing during a business trip, then make for the place du Casino in the very heart of Monte Carlo. Visit the Casino itself and take time to stroll around the gardens that front it before exploring the multicoloured Terrasse du Casino, taking in its views over the harbour of Port Hercule. Lunch before or after should preferably be at the old-world Café de Paris.

1 DAY: TIME TO SEE A LITTLE MORE

If you have more than half a day, then you can add on some contrasting sightseeing in the old town of Monaco-Ville. It's easy to reach the far end of the Rocher de Monaco (Rock of Monaco) (buses 1 & 2 terminate there). Wander through the narrow streets, which seem to inhabit a different time and place from the glitz and bustle of Monte-Carlo. Don't forget to emerge at Jardins St-Martin on the south side of the Rock for great views over the coast and harbour of Fontvieille, before continuing to the cathedral where Princess Grace is buried. End your stroll at the Place du Palais and take time out to tour the Palais Princier.

2–3 DAYS: TIME TO SEE MUCH MORE

With more time in hand you can visit some of the attractions in Monaco-Ville (especially the Oceanographic Museum) and on the nearby terrasses de Fontvieille, with its collections of vintage cars, scale-model ships and Monégasque stamps and coins. You should also make time to see the Jardin Exotique and Observatory Cave with its attendant museum of early mankind, or if you prefer, take the bus into Fontvieille and drink in the tranquillity of the Princess

Grace Rose Garden and the Parc Paysager, with its intriguing assembly of sculptures. While you're there you may want to take a helicopter tour from the nearby Héliport. This still leaves time during your stay for shopping in La Condamine (and, if your credit card allows, Monte Carlo's designer emporia), and you can fit in some self-indulgent physical refreshment at one of Monaco's spas or beauty and fitness centres. In the evenings, party in the nightclubs and bars of Monte Carlo, and the harbour front, or take in a show or a game of roulette at the Casino.

LONGER: ENJOYING MONACO TO THE FULL

You'll want to return to some of the places on the two–three day schedule, by day and night, but a longer visit gives you time to explore the lesser delights of the Principality. You can also take off from Monaco-Ville rail station for destinations along the Riviera, such as Menton and Ventimiglia.

● *There are many great places to explore on the Riviera, such as Menton*

Something for nothing

Despite its pricey reputation, you don't have to bankrupt yourself to enjoy Monaco and, although there is an entrance fee to most attractions (usually a fairly modest one), many of its best experiences come at little or no charge.

For such a built-up area, Monaco offers some excellent walking, both in its beautifully maintained parks and open spaces (all free) and out along the coastal paths of the Riviera, either southwards, from Fontvieille to Cap d'Ail, or north from Monte Carlo Beach to Cap-Martin, both taking about three hours there and back along the villa-studded shoreline. Football fans will have an extra treat if they take the 40-minute walk along Monaco's own shore, from Monte

CHEMIN DES SCULPTURES (SCULPTURE TRAIL)

As you stroll through Monaco, you can't fail to notice the modern sculptures that adorn the streets. Some of them are grotesque, some hilarious, some poignant, and many of them truly beautiful works of art. Together they represent a massive, free-of-charge outdoor exhibition of the work of the world's best-known modern sculptors. The full trail, comprising 90 works in all, extends the whole length of the Principality, from Larvotto beach to Fontvieille, though the greatest concentration is to be found around the Parc Paysager and Princess Grace Rose Garden in Fontvieille (see page 103). You can even get an illustrated guide to them all from the tourist office. Following the trail makes a great themed walking tour of Monaco that won't cost you a penny.

Carlo Beach to Port Hercule: the footprints of the world's most famous footballers have been moulded into the ground along the way – see if you can spot Roberto Baggio, Pelé, Alfredo Di Stefano, Michel Platini and George Best.

The medieval streets of the old town are a walker's and photographer's delight, and they all end eventually on an edge of the Rocher de Monaco, the promontory on which Monaco-Ville is built, looking out to great views of the two harbours and the Riviera coast.

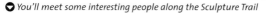
You'll meet some interesting people along the Sculpture Trail

When it rains

There won't be many days when rain stops play in Monaco, but if you are sheltering from a stiff breeze or a half-day downpour, there are plenty of indoor attractions. The resort's museums are varied and have something for every interest and age group. You could easily spend a morning or afternoon in the Oceanographic Museum (see page 84), with its shark tank and other aquaria; the Palais Princier and its attendant museums (page 81) likewise make a good half-day visit, and if your interests run that way, it's easy to lose track of time in the Maritime Museum (page 106) or Classic Car Exhibition (page 105).

Alternatively, get under cover in the Métropole shopping centre in Monte Carlo (see page 67) and shop till you drop – you can always window shop if the price tags are too high, and it has plenty of cafés and bars where you can people-watch.

If the weather is wet, why not get wet anyway? Monaco is rich in high-quality swimming pools, such as the Stade Nautique Rainier III (see page 99) and the Stade Louis II in Fontvieille (page 104). Or make this the day to treat yourself to some self-indulgent pampering in one of the area's excellent spas, such as the Thermes Marins (see page 77), or work yourself to fitness in their well-equipped gyms.

If that all sounds too much like hard work, simply find a cosy table at the Café de Paris or another high temple of cuisine and sample some of the best cooking on the Continent. And don't forget, the casinos are always open.

● *When it rains it's good to get underwater at the Oceanographic Museum*

On arrival

TIME DIFFERENCES

Monaco's clocks follow Central European Time (CET). During Daylight Saving Time (end Mar–end Oct), the clocks are put ahead one hour.

ARRIVING

By air

The air gateway to Monaco is 25 km (15 miles) away at Nice-Côte d'Azur Airport. The airport is the second largest in France in terms of passengers (8 million a year) but it's a manageable size and gets its customers landside pretty quickly. In each of the two terminals there are two banks to take care of any foreign exchange needs, open 08.00–22.00 all year.

The coolest, fastest and most expensive way to get from the airport to Monaco is by helicopter. Flights depart every 20 minutes direct from the airport to Monaco's heliport, taking just seven minutes for a one-way fare of €75 (prior reservation is a good idea). From the heliport, a shuttle bus will take you to your hotel.

Héliport ⓐ av. des Ligures ⓣ 92 05 00 50 ⓦ www.heliairmonaco.com ⓛ 70 flights daily

More mundane ways to get from either terminal include taxi (average 35 minutes and, at €70, not much cheaper than the helicopter), bus (bus line Rapide Côte d'Azur; about 50 minutes, fare €13 ⓦ www.rca.tm.fr ⓛ 09.00–21.00), or train, which is cheap, but probably the least convenient method, as it's a 500-yard walk from the airport terminal to St Augustin station, from where local TER train will get you to Nice-Ville station in about 20 minutes, and very frequent trains from Nice-Ville take you to Monte Carlo in 30 minutes.

Car-hire firms at the airport include ADA, Avis, Budget, Europcar, Hertz, National/Alamo and Sixt; the pick-up point is outside

▲ *Arrive in style at the héliport*

Terminal 2 (reached from Terminal 1 via free shuttle bus).
Nice-Côte d'Azur Airport ☎ flight information 0820 423 333
🌐 www.nice.aeroport.fr

By rail
The international SNCF rail station is located at av. Prince-Pierre in
the Condamine district, which is where the majority of 2- and 3-star
hotels are clustered. It's a short taxi ride from there to the other
districts. This new sub-surface station has replaced the Ancienne
Gare in the middle of town as the main arrival point.

By road
The France–Italy A8 motorway skirts Monaco. If approaching from
the west turn off at junction 56, signposted Monaco, or from the
east at the Monaco-Roquebrune exit. If you don't mind sharp bends,
leave the motorway earlier and get onto the Moyenne Corniche

coastal road for great views. There are plenty of car parks within Monaco; many of the smaller hotels don't have their own parking but are seldom far away from a large public car park.

By water

Cruise ships dock at Port Hercule, right in the middle of Monaco, flanked by the rock of Monaco-Ville on one side and Monte Carlo on the other. There are plenty of buses from the harbour to Monte Carlo and Monaco-Ville (in fact, you can just hop on a lift to take you to the latter).

FINDING YOUR FEET

Monaco puts itself out to be helpful to visitors, and in a city so small it's hard to get lost. The presence of so much money ensures that streets are safe and clean, with few undesirable characters, and there are plenty of policemen on hand. Make sure you don't unwittingly cause problems. You don't have to dress glamorously but you should try to look respectable: bare chests, bare feet and swimwear are illegal in public anywhere but the beach. And don't upset the gendarmes by crossing against traffic signals or away from authorised pedestrian crossings.

◌ *The Moyenne Corniche is the scenic approach to Monaco*

ORIENTATION

Monaco is basically a small strip of coastline bordered on all sides by France. Its two harbours, the main Port Hercule (also called Port de Monaco) and the smaller yacht harbour of Port de Fontvieille, divide the coastline into three distinct areas. Jutting out between the two ports is the rocky plateau of the old town; the correct name for this quarter is simply Monaco, but to avoid confusion with the Principality as a whole it is referred to throughout this book by its alternative name of Monaco-Ville (it is also known as the Rocher de Monaco, the Rock of Monaco). Dominated by the Palais Princier (Prince's Palace, see page 78) and distinguished by its elegant 18th-century houses

---

IF YOU GET LOST, TRY ...

Excuse me, do you speak English?
Excusez-moi, parlez-vous anglais?
Ekskeweh mwah, pahrlay-voo ohnglay?

Excuse me, is this the right way to the old town/the city centre/the tourist office/the station/the bus station?
Excusez-moi, c'est la bonne direction pour la vieille ville/ au centre-ville/l'office de tourisme/la gare/gare routière?
Ekskewzaymwah, seh lah bon deerekseeawng poor lah veeay veel/oh sahngtr veel/lohfeece de tooreezm/lah gahr/gahr rootyair?

Can you point to it on my map?
Pouvez-vous me le montrer sur la carte?
Poovehvoo mer ler mawngtreh sewr lah kart?

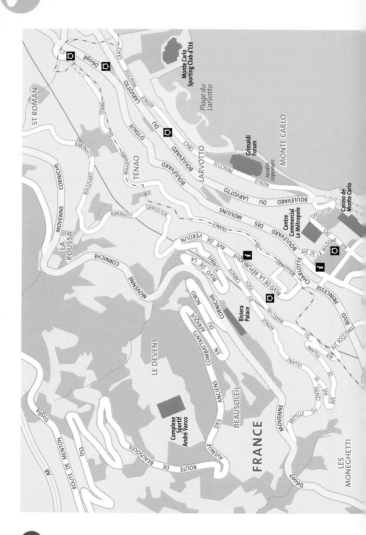

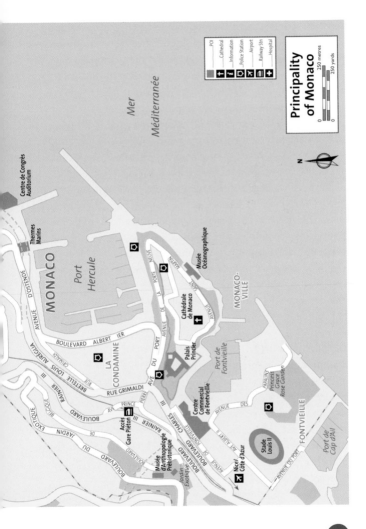

Principality of Monaco

	POI
✝	Cathedral
ℹ	Information
🛡	Police Station
✈	Airport
🚉	Railway Stn
✚	Hospital

0 — 250 metres
0 — 250 yards

N

Mer Méditerranée

Centre de Congrès Auditorium

Thermes Marins

MONACO

Port Hercule

Musée Océanographique

AVENUE D'OSTENDE

BOULEVARD ALBERT IER

LA CONDAMINE

Cathédrale de Monaco

MONACO-VILLE

BRETELLE LOUIS AURÉGLIA

RUE GRIMALDI

AVE DU PORT

Palais Princié

Port de Fontvieille

BOULEVARD RAINIER III

JARDIN EXOTIQUE

AVENUE PRINCE PIERRE

Accès Gare Piéton

BOULEVARD CHARLES III

RUE PRINCESSE CAROLINE

Centre Commercial de Fontvieille

PRINCESSE Grace Rose Garden

Musée d'Anthropologie Préhistorique

Jardin Exotique

Nice/Côte d'Azur

BOULEVARD DE BELGIQUE

AVE ALBERT II

AVENUE DES

FONTVIEILLE

Stade Louis II

Port de Cap d'Ail

painted in pastel shades, Monaco-Ville is the original area of the Principality and is still where the oldest native Monégasque families live. Facing Monaco-Ville, across the smaller harbour to which it gives its name, is the newest district, largely built on reclaimed land, the suburb of Fontvieille. This is mainly a residential area of high-rise, high-priced apartments, but it possesses some visitor attractions too, such as the Princess Grace Rose Garden (see pages 103–4). North of Port Hercule is Monte Carlo, created in 1866 by, and named after, Prince Charles III, which is the glamorous end of the city, home to the Casino and other high-society hotels, bars and restaurants.

At the centre of inland Monaco, extending back from Port Hercule, lies La Condamine. The second-oldest area of Monaco (the name refers to the cultivated land that originally supplied the needs of the castle), this is a district of hotels and shops, which also contains the railway and bus stations. Behind La Condamine the suburb of Moneghetti climbs up into the hillside. North along the coast beyond Monte Carlo lies Larvotto, extending from its separate bay, with Monaco's largest beach, back to the national border with the French municipality of Roquebrune.

GETTING AROUND

The entire coastline of Monaco is just over 4 km (2 1/2 miles) in length, and the city extends inland an average 1 km (just over 1/2 mile). It is therefore quite feasible to visit most of what the city has to offer on foot. The steepness of its coastal geography would be a drawback for pedestrian sightseeing if it weren't for the public lifts (elevators) that the considerate Monégasque authorities have provided. Seven of them are currently in use, in the following locations:

- Place des Moulins
- Princess Grace Hospital Center – Jardin Exotique

- Harbour – av. de la Costa
- Place Ste-Dévote – Moneghetti
- Casino terraces – Congress Centre Auditorium – blvd Louis II
- av. des Citronniers – av. Grande-Bretagne
- blvd Rainier III – blvd de Larvotto

In addition, there are many other escalators and moving walkways around town to ease you towards your destination.

Buses

For less energetic or longer travel around Monaco, there is a small but excellent bus system of just five lines (numbered 1, 2, 4, 5 and 6 – there's no Line 3) that carries over 5 million passengers a year. Lines 1 and 2 connect Monaco-Ville with Monte Carlo's Casino (Line 1 continues to St-Roman on the northern border). Lines 4 and 5 both connect the railway station with the city – 4 goes to Monte Carlo and on to Larvotto, 5 heads in the other direction to Fontvieille. Line 6 traverses the entire coastline from Fontvieille, via the main harbour and the Casino and on to Larvotto. Buses run every 11 minutes, 07.00–21.00 Mon–Sat; every 20 minutes 07.30–21.00 Sun & public holidays. Flat-fare tickets (€1.00) are purchased on the bus from the driver; you can buy singles or multi-trip (10 journeys), or a Day Travel Card (€3.60) for an unlimited day's use of the buses.

Compagnie des Autobus de Monaco ⓐ 3 av. Président J F Kennedy, 98000 Monaco ❶ 97 70 22 22 Ⓦ www.cam.mc

Taxis

Taxis are available 24 hours daily by calling ❶ 93 15 01 01. There are also taxi ranks at the exits to the rail station, the Casino, av. des Papalins in Fontvieille, near the Hotel Méridien Beach Plaza in Larvotto, av. du Président Kennedy at the port, and several other strategic points

around Monaco. The average fare for travelling within Monaco is
€10 during the day and €12 at night.

If you are in a party of more than four, consider hiring a minibus
taxi, an 8–13-seater vehicle, from the Station Tulip Inn Terminus.

Station Tulip Inn Terminus av. Prince-Pierre 🕿 92 05 25 57

Trains

TER (regional French railway) trains from the central railway station
(🅐 av. Prince-Pierre, La Condamine) provide an easy, and remarkably
cheap, way to visit the Riviera beyond Monaco. There are at least
20 trains a day in both directions, allowing quick access east to
Menton (approx. 12 mins) and the Italian town of Ventimiglia
(24 mins) and west to Nice (25 mins) and many other resorts, as far
as Cannes (1 hr 10 mins). Not all trains stop at every station on the
line, so pick up a free timetable. Tickets can be purchased at easy-to-
use machines at all stops. If you fancy a day of Riviera-hopping, quite
feasible given the short journey times, you can save money with an
Isabelle Card (€12), which gives you a day's unlimited travel on the
regional service between St Raphael in the west and Ventimiglia
in the east (July–Sept only).

SNCF reservation and information 🕿 92 35 35 35
🕸 www.ter-sncf.com/paca

Driving

Driving within the centre of Monaco could be slower than walking,
but if you are staying outside the centre and driving in every day,
you won't find any shortage of car parks, many of them with CCTV
surveillance. On-street parking is restricted and the gendarmes are
very fussy about not only where you park but how tidily you park!
Monaco roads operate on a one-way system, so finding your way

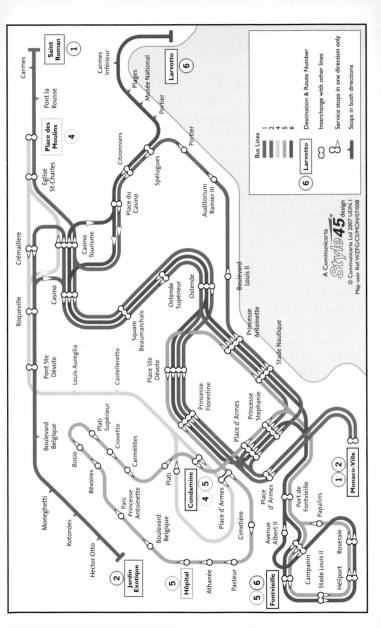

can be a little tricky even for seasoned drivers. Note that access by car to Monaco-Ville is restricted to cars registered in Monaco or the Alpes-Maritimes *département* of France.

CAR HIRE

If you want to hire a car, it's usually better and cheaper to do it in advance through your travel agent, airline or one of the main auto rental companies' central booking systems on the web. If it's a spur-of-the-moment decision, Avis, Hertz and Europcar, and five local companies, have offices in Monaco itself – the tourist office can provide a full list. For airport car rentals, see page 50.

You may want to hire a chauffeur-driven limo to turn up at the Casino or the Café de Paris – so much more impressive than getting off the bus. Since this is Monaco, there are no less than 11 companies providing this service (details from tourist office or your hotel).

Or perhaps you want to live a fantasy millionaire lifestyle for a day or two (and this is certainly the place to do it); you can hire a swanky self-drive limousine or sports car from:

Elite Rent a Car ⓐ 34 quai Jean-Charles-Rey ⓣ 97 77 33 11 ⓦ www.eliterent.com

● *Monaco perches precariously between mountain and sea*

THE CITY & PRINCIPALITY OF
Monaco

Monte Carlo

This is the district that has made Monaco famous; the very name conjures up images of fortunes being won and lost at the gambling tables in surroundings of unparalleled luxury. The original name, Plateau des Spélugues, would never have had the same ring to it. It was Charles III who, having decided to repair the state's fortunes by one of history's earliest large-scale leisure developments, named the area after himself – 'Charles' Hill' in Italian. It could be argued that the other Charles who is commemorated in the name is the French architect Charles Garnier. Monte Carlo is dominated by the buildings Garnier designed, including not only the Casino and Opera House but also the impressive Musée National.

CHARLES GARNIER

Charles Garnier (1825–1898) was born of humble origins in Paris. After working his way up as a draughtsman he entered the Ecole des Beaux-Arts, and studied for five years at the Academy in Rome, gaining inspiration from the grandeur of ancient Roman architecture. While still a humble municipal architect, Garner entered and won the competition to design the new Paris Opéra in 1861. His vision, marked by drama, colour and decorative detail, reflected the grandiose aspirations of Napoleon III's Second Empire and his career never looked back. Garnier quickly became the architect of choice for large prestige projects of the period and was eagerly sought by his namesake, Charles III of Monaco, to create the impressive array of public buildings that still characterise Monte Carlo.

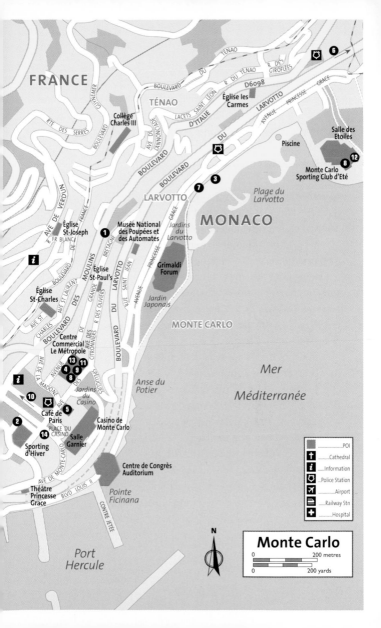

The westernmost suburb of Monaco, Larvotto, is in many ways an extension of Monte Carlo and is included in this chapter. It has few attractions of its own but is blessed with a large beach, and its nightlife is centred on the large and upmarket Le Sporting Club.

SIGHTS & ATTRACTIONS

Casino de Monte Carlo

Built by Garnier in 1878, the world's most famous temple to the Goddess of Fortune would be an attraction even without the glamour of what goes on inside. The impressive facade is set off by a large garden of flowerbeds and ponds surrounded by manicured lawns, extending from the front of the Casino gently upwards towards the town. At the rear is an even larger multicoloured terrace of geometric patterns designed by the artist Vasarely, which forms the roof of the Convention Centre and Auditorium below, and is part of Monaco's Sculpture Trail (see pages 46 and 103).

Opulent is the only way to describe the Casino's interior, with its wealth of gold leaf, ornate plasterwork, frescoes and sculptures. The marble-paved atrium is surrounded by 28 Ionic columns in onyx. It leads into the recently renovated Salle Garnier, the red-and-gold auditorium of the Opéra, which opened in 1879 with a performance by Sarah Bernhardt and has been the scene of international-class performances of opera, ballet and concerts ever since.

The gaming area of the Casino consists a succession of rooms featuring stained-glass windows, admirable decorations and sculptures, allegorical paintings and bronze lamps.

If you want to visit the Casino, rather than play there, it still pays to dress smartly (jacket and tie obligatory for men). It costs nothing to visit, though.

ⓐ pl. du Casino ⓣ 98 06 21 21 ⓦ www.casino-monte-carlo.com
ⓛ From 12.00 (see page 71 for the gaming schedules) Ⓝ Bus: 1, 2, 6
to Casino

Église St-Charles (St Charles' Church)

A few blocks away from the Casino, at the very edge of Monte Carlo
and of the Principality, stands the church that Charles III built for his
patron saint in 1883 in a style officially described as French Renaissance.
(The dearth of authentic medieval churches is a reminder of how
recent the origins of Monaco's wealth are.) Its highlights include
the 36 m (108 ft) bell tower, 19 stained-glass windows and the
gilded chandeliers, which used to decorate the Palace Throne Room.
ⓐ av. Saint-Charles ⓣ 93 30 74 90 ⓛ Daily Ⓝ Bus: 1, 4 to St Charles

Grimaldi Forum

The Grimaldi Forum's original purpose as a super-luxurious conference
centre has been somewhat eclipsed by its popularity as a nightlife
destination, with its young and glamorous nightclub the Karément
and hip bar Zebra Square. The Grimaldi forum hosts a number of
star-studded awards ceremonies and its many superb exhibitions
often spill out onto its seafront terrace. ⓐ 10 av. Princesse Grace
ⓣ 99 99 21 00 ⓦ www.grimaldiforum.com Ⓝ Bus: 6 to Musée National

Jardin Japonais (Japanese Garden)

Follow the winding avenue des Spélugues around the garden of the
Casino onto the avenue Princesse Grace to reach the Japanese Garden,
an oasis of serenity that is spiritually a million miles from the glitz
of Casino Square. Designed by the landscape architect Yasuo Beppu,
the garden is a living work of art that covers 2,300 sq m (25,000 sq ft)
and has been blessed by a Shinto High Priest. Stone, water and plants

The Jardin Japonais provides some welcome tranquillity in Monte Carlo

have been combined in the harmony for which the Japanese garden design is famous. In early spring look out for the flowering of the wealth of azaleas, rhododendrons and camellias.

🅐 av. Princesse Grace 🕑 09.00–sunset Ⓝ Bus: 6 to Portier

Musée National des Automates et Poupées
(National Museum of Automatons and Dolls)

Doll museums are not uncommon, but Monaco's must be one of the most sophisticated. The core of this museum is the ingenuity of Parisian toymakers in the 19th century, when highly crafted moving figures were the ultimate in 'too-good-to-give-the-children' presents. The exhibits are displayed in showcases complete with miniature furniture. The automatons are demonstrated daily to visitors. The collection is housed in another Garnier building, set in a terraced rose garden. 🅐 17 av. Princesse Grace 🕐 98 98 91 26 🅦 www.monte-

carlo.mc/musee-national ⏱ 10.00–18.30 except public holidays and
during Grand Prix, Easter–Sept; 10.00–12.15,14.30–18.30 Oct–Easter
🚍 Bus: 6 to Musée National. Admission charge

Place du Casino (Casino Square)

The square is the place to see celebrities, real or wannabe, and the
seriously wealthy. This is the social hub of Monte Carlo, where high-
rollers alight from their chauffeur-driven sports cars and limousines.
The venerable Café de Paris flanks one side of the square, and the
Hôtel de Paris, one of the original luxury hotels built at the same
time as the Casino, faces it on the other side.

RETAIL THERAPY

For most of us, Monte Carlo will be more for window shopping than
actual purchases. The so-called 'Golden Square' of the avenue Monte
Carlo, avenue des Beaux-Arts and Allées Lumières are home to some
of the most famous names in fashion and design: Hermès, Céline,
Christian Dior, Yves St Laurent, Louis Vuitton, Gucci, Chanel, Prada,
Ichthys, the list goes on. Place du Casino and nearby streets major
on jewellery: Cartier, Chopard, Van Cleef & Arpels, Bulgari, Piaget are
just some of the names here. Antiques and fine arts, naturally, are
much in evidence, as well as stores displaying the very latest in
interior design and tableware. The Métropole shopping centre just
off the square has 80 or so boutiques, as well as cafés and bars
catering to weary shoppers.

This is also where you will find a branch of FNAC, the well-known
French chain that combines CDs, books and computers and other
electronic products with a ticket agency, and a supermarket for food
shopping. Away from the Casino area, towards the Église St-Charles

(see page 65) is where you will find the bakers, *charcutiers* and greengrocers of Monte Carlo.

TAKING A BREAK

Don't leave Monte Carlo without treating yourself to the comparatively inexpensive pleasure of sipping a cup of coffee in one of the cafés around place du Casino, on the terrace of the Café de Paris or in the Métropole shopping centre, while watching the comings and goings of Monaco's beautiful people. Also consider treating yourself to a superb lunch in any of the top hotels; it won't be cheap but it's a less expensive way than dinner to experience the very best of Monaco's haute cuisine.

Bar-Tabacs des Moulins £ ❶ It's tiny but somehow always manages to fit everyone in, the service is quick, and the food fresh and inexpensive. ❷ 46 blvd des Moulins ❸ 93 50 66 39 ❹ Daily ❺ Bus: 1, 4 to Place des Moulins

Häagen Dazs £ ❷ This famous company needs no introduction but its outdoor café in Monaco is situated in the gardens at the place du Casino. The surroundings and the staff are extremely charming. ❷ Place du Casino ❸ 93 30 38 30 ❹ 10.00–21.00 Mon–Fri, 10.00–23.00 Sat & Sun ❺ Bus: 1, 2, 4, 6 to Tourisme Casino

La Note Bleue £–££ ❸ Great summer-only daytime café and bar, perfect for lunch in between sunbathing sessions on Larvotto's beach (for which you can rent a deckchair from them). Tapas and live music by the beach. ❷ Plage Larvotto ❸ 93 50 05 02 ❹ 08.30–19.30 Apr–Sept. Closed Oct–Mar ❺ Bus: 6 to Plages

MetCafé £–££ ❹ This swanky bar and café offers gourmet snacks and sandwiches on the ground floor of the Métropole shopping gallery. ⓐ Centre Commercial le Métropole, 4 av. de la Madone ⓣ 93 25 86 10 ⓛ 09.00–19.00 Mon–Sat ⓝ Bus: 1, 4, 6 to Place du Casino

Café de Paris ££ ❺ The Café de Paris has been a Monaco landmark for over a hundred years. Its popularity is unrivalled and it remains the best place in town to sip an espresso while taking in the bustle around the Casino. ⓐ Place du Casino ⓣ 98 06 76 23 ⓛ 07.00–01.00 ⓝ Bus: 1, 2, 4, 6 to Tourisme Casino

La Vigie ££ ❻ This upmarket brasserie at the SBM-owned Monte Carlo Beach Hotel is technically not in Monte Carlo or even in Monaco, and it's certainly not a low-cost option, but if you like a really good Sunday brunch it's the place to go (the in-crowd usually arrive by yacht). ⓐ av. Princess Grace, Roquebrune ⓣ 98 06 52 52 ⓦ www.montecarloresort.com ⓝ Take a taxi – or hire a yacht

AFTER DARK

Monte Carlo is where Monaco's nightlife begins and ends. You can mix with the glamorous crowd at the Casino and other fashionable hangouts for the price of a drink, though to feel really comfortable you'll want to wear your smartest evening wear – casual is fine (except at the Casino) but make it very chic-casual if you want to blend in.

Remember, whatever your intentions, if you want to play at a casino you need to be over 21 and to have your passport or national identity card with you. Minimum dress code for gentlemen is a sports jacket and tie. No specific code for ladies, but you might want to observe arrivals the night before to check out what the competition is wearing.

If you're a roulette novice, see page 31 for the different styles; you can download full rules from the Casino website (see opposite).

Café de Paris American roulette, craps, blackjack and slot machines and video poker in the venerable Café's three gaming rooms.
ⓐ pl. du Casino ☏ 98 06 76 23 ⏱ From 10.00 (slots);
16.00 (video poker); 17.00 (roulette and card tables)

Casino de Monte Carlo The Casino is divided into rooms according to your taste, all with admission charges of €10–20 per person. Slot

THE MAN WHO BROKE THE BANK AT MONTE CARLO

A popular British music-hall song of 1892 with this title was inspired by the exploits of English gambler Charles Wells. But it was his fellow-countryman Joseph Jaggers who really did break the bank at Monte Carlo, 20 years earlier. An engineer in the mills of Victorian Yorkshire, he arrived in Monte Carlo in 1873 determined to prove that roulette wheels, being just machines, could be beaten. After compiling a mass of statistics on the roll of the wheels, he identified nine numbers that regularly came up on one of the six wheels in use at the casino, owing to a slight imbalance in its mechanism. He proceeded to bet heavily on them and on his first night cleared nearly £50,000. The Casino switched wheels between tables overnight but he soon identified the imperfect one and continued to win. Eventually he won over £250,000, making him a multi-millionaire in today's money. Sadly, he died in poverty in the year the song came out.

machines are in the *Salle Blanche* (White Room), French and English roulette and *trente et quarante* can be found in the *Salle Europe* and craps and blackjack in the *Salle des Amériques* (American Room). The *Salons Privés* (private rooms) offer English and European roulette, *chemin de fer* and other more abstruse games, but for high rollers only. ⓐ pl. du Casino ☏ 98 06 21 21 ⓦ www.casinomontecarlo.com ⏰ Salle Blanche: from 14.00 Mon–Fri, from 12.00 Sat & Sun. Salles Europe & des Amériques: from 12.00. Also consult the casino website for more detail ⓝ Bus: 1, 2, 4, 6 to Casino Tourisme. Arrival by taxi or hired limo is more the done thing, however.

Jimmy'z The legendary nightclub and disco at Le Sporting attracts models, pop stars and the rich and famous in general, so be prepared to dress the part and pay the prices. ☏ 98 06 70 61 (before 23.00); 98 06 70 68 (after 23.00) ⏰ 23.30–dawn Wed–Sun, Nov–Easter ⓝ Bus: 6 to Carmes Inférieur

Salle des Etoiles The big-name acts perform here, and when the event is advertised as a Gala Evening (often in aid of charity), everyone who is anyone in Monaco will be there (and the dress code steps up a notch). ☏ 98 06 36 36 (reservations 10.00–19.00) ⏰ 20.30 for dinner, 22.45 for the show. Check what's on when in the tourist office listings or on its website ⓝ Bus: 6 to Carmes Inférieur

Salle des Palmiers is part of Le Sporting (see below) and is the only gaming room with a sea view. Same games as at the Casino de Monte Carlo, except that American roulette is also played.

Le Sporting In a category of its own for nightlife, on account of its many facets, the Sporting Club de Monaco is always in fashion. Dine, sip cocktails, dance till dawn, enjoy acts from world-famous stars, or lose your shirt at the roulette tables – it's your choice and they're not mutually exclusive options either. You could pack the equivalent of two very full nights out into one evening at Le Sporting. ❸ av. Princess Grace, on its own promontory facing Larvotto beach at the northern end of the Principality.

Sun Casino Once owned by an independent hotel, the Sun Casino has since merged with the great SBM monopoly, even though the hotel it's housed in hasn't. Its collection of slot machines is 435 strong and you'll find craps, blackjack as well as Roulette Américaine tables (see page 31). ❸ Fairmont Monte Carlo Hotel, 12 av. des Spélugues ❶ 93 50 65 00 ❷ From 11.00 (slots); 17.00 Mon–Fri, 16.00 Sat & Sun (tables)

RESTAURANTS

The relatively tiny area of Monte Carlo probably has more restaurants than most big European cities, so any selection is just the tip of the iceberg, and there are plenty more than this to discover. Though the area is not given over entirely to haute cuisine, that's what it's best known for.

Baobab £ ❼ Cheap and very cheerful brasserie, overlooking the Larvotto beach. ❸ av. Princesse Grace ❶ 93 50 86 90 ❷ 12.00–24.00 (closed Sat evenings) ⓝ Bus: 4, 6 to Larvotto

Fuji £–££ ❽ If your experience of Japanese food has been limited to sushi, this restaurant downstairs in the Métropole shopping complex will be a revelation and won't break the bank. Try one of the set menus if you're not familiar with the choices. There's another branch at

Le Sporting, but it's a bit more expensive to eat there. ⓐ Centre Commercial le Métropole, 4 av. de la Madone ⓣ 93 30 40 11 ⓛ 12.00–14.30 Tues–Sat, 20.00–22.30 Mon ⓝ Bus: 1, 2, 4, 6 to Casino Tourisme

Rampoldi Restaurant £–££ ❾ Affordable eating, given the area, with Italian specialities, in this long-established restaurant. ⓐ 2 av. des Spélugues ⓣ 93 30 70 65 ⓛ 12.00–14.00, 19.30–23.30 ⓝ Bus: 1, 2, 4, 6 to Casino Tourisme

Il Terrazzino ££ ❿ Authentic southern Italian cooking, especially good on antipasti and pasta, and the generous portions make this a good-value stop for a full lunch or dinner. A couple of blocks back from the Casino. ⓐ 2 rue des Iris ⓣ 93 50 24 27 ⓛ 10.30–14.30, 18.30–23.00 ⓝ Bus: 1, 2, 4, 6 to Casino Tourisme

Café de Paris ££–£££ ❺ Dining at the Café de Paris, right on the place du Casino, is a date with history. It can number the great Escoffier among its chefs – this is the kitchen in which he accidentally invented *crêpes suzettes* in 1898. Not that there's anything stuffy or old-fashioned about the food in this stylish brasserie, which does excellent cocktails and offers special menus on themes such as Provençal or Latin American cuisine from time to time. ⓐ pl. du Casino ⓣ 92 16 20 20 ⓝ Bus: 1, 2, 4, 6 to Casino Tourisme

Pacific ££–£££ ⓫ Pacific is the ultra-hip brainchild of the former manager of the glamorous Jimmy'z nightclub and one of the places to see and be seen in Monaco. The food is an elegant fusion of Japanese and Italian. ⓐ 17 av. des Spélugues ⓣ 93 25 20 30 ⓛ 12.00–14.00, 20.00–24.00 ⓝ Bus: 1, 2, 4, 6 to Casino Tourisme

Le Bar et Boeuf £££ ⑫ Lovingly prepared sea bass and beef dishes are the trademark at this upscale restaurant. The real trick in the summer is to stay until 23.00 and enjoy the Sporting Club's fireworks. ⓐ Le Sporting, av. Princesse Grace ⓣ 98 06 71 71 ⓛ 19.00–01.00, May–Sept. Booking essential for outdoor seating ⓝ Bus: 6 to Carmes Inférieur

Joël Robuchon £££ ⑬ Monaco's newly Michelin-starred restaurant Joël Robuchon is the Hôtel Métropole's crowning glory. Named after its famous chef, it is currently hot on the heels of the Louis XV for the title of best restaurant in the principality. The cuisine is modern, rich and sophisticated. ⓐ Hôtel Métropole, 4 av. de la Madone ⓣ 93 15 15 15 ⓛ 12.00–14.00, 20.00–24.00 ⓝ Bus: 1, 2, 4, 6 to Casino Tourisme

Louis XV £££ ⑭ The renowned restaurant of the Hôtel de Paris has one of the most glamorous terraces in the world and a dining room decorated in the style of Versailles. This was Alain Ducasse's first restaurant, though the chef de cuisine is now Franck Cerutti. You won't come across many better dining experiences, provided your wallet can take it (let the menu on the website tempt you). ⓐ Hôtel de Paris, pl. du Casino ⓣ 92 16 30 01 ⓦ www.alain-ducasse.com ⓛ 12.00–14.00 Thur–Mon, 19.00–22.00 ⓝ Bus: 1, 2, 4, 6 to Casino Tourisme

CAFÉS, BARS & CLUBS

Karément Currently the trendiest bar and club in Monaco, Karément boasts modern neon décor and an army of devoted followers. There is a club entrance fee on Friday and Saturday but the rest of the week is free. Thursday night is Salsa night. ⓐ Grimaldi Forum, 10 av. Princesse Grace ⓣ 99 99 20 20 ⓛ 11.00–dawn ⓝ Bus: 4, 6 to Larvotto

McCarthy's Pub Not all of Monte Carlo is exclusive and image-obsessed, and McCarthy's provides the friendly and lively atmosphere of a typical Irish bar, with live music, a DJ and all the Guinness you can drink. Locals happily mix with the occasional celebrity seeking refuge from the glitz. ⓐ 7 rue du Portier ⓣ 93 25 87 67 ⓛ 18.00–dawn ⓝ Bus: 6 to Portier

Sabor di Vino This cosy bar's passion for wine is infectious, they even bring you a free platter of tasty delicacies to help bring out your wine's subtler flavours. ⓐ Sabor di Vino, Galerie Charles III ⓣ 93 50 65 03 ⓛ 23.00–dawn ⓝ Bus: 1, 2, 6 to Ostende or Ostende Supérieur

Zebra Square Sophisticated bar with a dancing area. Enjoy a cocktail under the stars on the fantastic terrace then pop downstairs to Karément for some more serious boogying. ⓐ Grimaldi Forum, 10 av. Princesse Grace ⓣ 99 99 25 50 ⓛ 11.00–03.00 ⓝ Bus: 4, 6 to Larvotto

SHOWS & ENTERTAINMENT
Opera and concerts
In the winter season, you can enjoy classic and contemporary opera productions at the Salle Garnier, part of the Casino complex (see page 64) and at the Grimaldi Forum (see page 65). At any time of year it's worth checking with the tourist office to see what pop and orchestral concerts are taking place at the Grimaldi Forum and other Monte Carlo venues. ⓦ www.visitmonaco.com (go to 'Events' for a full calendar)

Cabaret du Casino ⓣ 98 06 22 00 ⓦ www.montecarloresort.com

Salle des Etoiles Located in the summer Sporting club, the Salle des Etoiles is the most prestigious concert venue in Monaco and showcases world-renowned talent every night during the summer. Tickets are expensive but the show is unique, with a three-course meal and fireworks to finish. ❷ Sporting d'été, 26 av. Princesse Grace ❶ 98 06 36 36 ❹ Check the website for specific events; 20.30 dinner, followed by variety acts at 22.45 ❹ Bus: 4, 6 to Larvotto

RELAXATION

PLAGE DU LARVOTTO

The Plage du Larvotto is strictly speaking the only beach in Monaco. The many others lie on or just beyond the border. Much of this free beach is now sectioned off semi-private areas, where you can rent deckchairs and order food and cocktails to be brought to you. The best of these areas is the Note Bleue (see page 68). A quarter of an hour's walk down the same street leads you to its snazzy sister the 'Monte Carlo Beach', where you'll pay €50 for entry. If you want to have a look around first, say you're just going to its (excellent) Sea Lounge bar, which has free entry and worth a visit in its own right. ❷ beach access from av. Princesse Grace ❹ Bus: 6 to Plages

SPAS, BEAUTY SALONS & FITNESS CENTRES

Monte Carlo offers its visitors a wealth of facilities to help them feel good and look good. Other establishments offer a wide range of beauty treatments, keep-fit programmes and massage. Here are just a few.

Beauty Spa Daniela Steiner Manicure, pedicure, anticellulite treatment, facial care and slimming programmes. ❷ 1 av. de Grande Bretagne ❶ 97 77 13 66

Centre de Fitness Trained staff using state-of-the-art equipment will put you through your own tailor-made fitness programme.
🄐 Fairmont Monte Carlo Hotel, 12 av. des Spélugues 🕿 93 50 65 00

Institut de Soins Jacques Dessange Scalp, face and body treatments, using massage with coloured clays and oils. 🄐 5 blvd des Moulins 🕿 97 97 39 29

Monte Carlo Gym Aerobics gym, body-building and stretching.
🄐 6 blvd des Moulins 🕿 93 25 85 58

Sunshine Yoga Private and group classes in yoga of all kinds.
🄐 1 av. Henry Dunant 🕿 06 64 91 96 42

Thermes Marins If you're looking for the ultimate in pampering, or want expert help easing aches and pains, then the Thermes Marins, recently voted one of the best three health spas in the world, is for you. Facing onto the sea and just round the corner from the Hôtel de Paris and the Casino, it offers every kind of health, relaxation and beauty treatment: seawater therapies such as calming marine baths and hydromassage, hi-tech cardio training, an enormous swimming pool, a solarium, hammam and sauna – you name it, they provide it. Le Salon Bleu is a combined beauty and hairdressing salon, L'Hirondelle restaurant serves up low-calorie gastronomy, and you can stock up on vitamins with one of the Atlantide bar's cocktails. To get the full benefit, you should sign up for a six- or seven-day programme, but there are also one-day sessions. 🄐 2 av. de Monte Carlo 🕿 98 06 69 00 🌐 www.montecarlospa.com 🕐 08.00–20.00 (reception)

Monaco-Ville

This most conservative of the districts of Monaco is the home of the reigning family and most of the oldest-established Monégasque families. Its 86 m (280 ft) high rocky outcrop was the site of the old Ghibelline castle (now replaced by the Palais Princier – see page 81), where the first Grimaldi ruler founded his family's 700-year reign. The layout is medieval, with narrow streets and alleys opening onto small squares and fountains. It is the cultural and religious heart of Monaco, and the traditional Provençal architecture of the buildings and Catholic churches reflect this.

SIGHTS & ATTRACTIONS

Cathédrale de Monaco

Leaving the place du Palais at its southern end by the rue Col. Bellando de Castro, it's a short walk to Monaco's cathedral. Built in 1875, like much of modern Monaco in the white stone from nearby la Turbie, the neo-Romanesque cathedral stands on the site of a 13th-century chapel of St Nicholas. Here, among the tombs of other Grimaldi princes and princesses, you will find the simple slab that marks the tomb of Princess Grace. The Cathedral is also noteworthy for its altarpiece of St Nicholas, the work of Louis Bréa in 1500, and the impressive modern four-keyboard organ, which dates from 1976.

ⓐ 4 rue Col. Bellando de Castro ❶ 93 30 87 70 ❸ Daily
Ⓦ www.cathedrale.mc ❷ Bus: 1, 2 to Monaco Ville

Chapelle de la Miséricorde (Chapel of Mercy)

Built in 1639, the chapel was founded by the Order of Black Penitents. It houses a collection of religious art, including a wooden sculpture

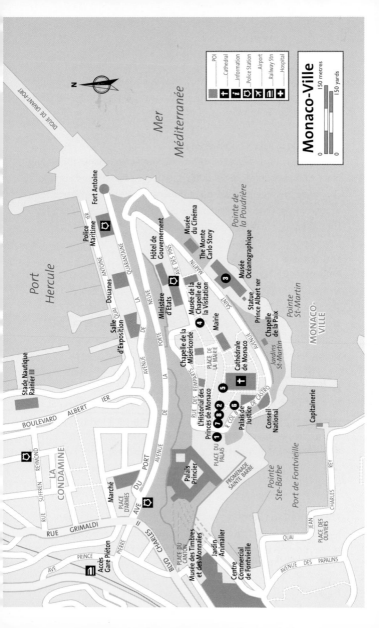

of Christ by François-Joseph Bosio, the Monaco-born official sculptor to the Emperor Napoléon I. ❸ pl. de la Mairie ⏰ Daily ⓝ Bus: 1, 2 to Monaco Ville

Chapelle de la Paix (Chapel of Peace)

Within the Jardins St-Martin stands this tiny white chapel, the resting place of Prince Pierre, father of the late Prince Rainier, and Stefano Casiraghi, the second husband of Princess Caroline, who was killed in 1990 in a speedboat accident while defending his World Offshore title. ⓝ Bus: 1, 2 to Monaco Ville

Fort Antoine

This early 18th-century fortress stands on the very end of the Rock of Monaco-Ville. It is now used as an open-air theatre with a capacity of 350 spectators in tiered seating built in a semi-circle, an atmospheric setting for evening performances during the summer. ❸ av. de la Quarantaine ❶ 93 15 80 00 ⏰ Daily except during performances ⓝ Bus: 1, 2 to Monaco Ville

Jardins St-Martin (St Martin's Gardens)

Facing the Cathedral is the western end of the long garden that overlooks Fontvieille harbour. This 19th-century park of Aleppo pines and exotic plants was a favourite haunt of the poet Apollinaire. It is decorated with bronze statues, including a modern one of Prince Albert I, the guiding spirit behind the Oceanographic Institute, whose museum is located in the middle of the park (see page 84).

The Monte Carlo Story

This is the history of the Principality and its development into one of the world's leading pleasure capitals, told in a 35-minute film, with simultaneous translation into English and five other languages. There is also a small museum of cinema posters of films that have featured Monte Carlo as a backdrop. ⓐ Terrasses du Parking du Chemin des Pêcheurs ⓣ 93 25 32 33 ⓛ 14.00–18.00 July & Aug; 14.00–17.00 Jan–June, Sept & Oct ⓝ Bus: 1, 2 to Monaco Ville. Admission charge

Palais Princier (Prince's Palace)

Built on the site of the 13th-century castle of François Grimaldi, the Palais has been extended several times, particularly during the Renaissance. At its heart is an immense square, the Cour d'Honneur, paved with 3 million coloured pebbles in immense geometric patterns;

◆ *Palais Princier has been the Grimaldi power base for centuries*

concerts are held here during the summer. Dominating the Cour is an imposing 17th-century horseshoe-shaped double staircase made of Carrara marble. Behind the staircase is the Galerie à l'Italienne, a long gallery linking the state apartments, decorated with 16th-century Genoese frescoes of mythological scenes. These include the yellow and gold Louis XV Salon, the blue and gold Salon Bleu, and the Mazarin Salon, decorated with coloured wooden panels. The real highlight, however, is the impressive Salon du Trône (Throne Room) and its Renaissance fireplace. Audio-guided tours of the palace, available whenever the Prince is not in residence, take in all these sights. One wing of the palace houses the state archives and Napoleonic Museum (see page 83). The Palace's Sainte-Marie Tower is a more modern addition, built by Albert I in the early 20th century; this is where the Prince's red and white standard is flown when he is in residence. ⓐ pl. du Palais ⓣ 93 25 18 31 ⓦ www.palais.mc ⓛ 09.30–18.00 June–Sept; 10.00–17.00 Oct–Apr ⓝ Bus: 1, 2 to Monaco Ville. Admission charge for 30-min tour

Le Petit Train (part of the Azur Express)

This little red and white train takes you on a short tour around Monaco. Aside from being the most adorable thing in town, it also conducts a half-hour trip around the main areas of touristic interest in the Principality. It goes slowly, giving everyone a chance to enjoy the sights and the sun on the way. ⓐ Departure and arrivals outside the Oceanographic Institute (see page 84) ⓣ 92 05 64 38 ⓛ 10.30–17.00 ⓝ Bus: 1, 2 to Monaco Ville. Admission charge

Place du Palais (Palace Square)

The large square in front of the Palais Princier is lined with bronze cannons, a thoughtful gift from Monaco's ally Louis XIV of France.

The panoramas from all sides of the square offer views as far as Italy. At 11.55 every day the Prince's guard of carabiniers (uniformed in black during the winter, white in summer) perform the 100-year-old ceremony of the Changing of the Guard in front of the Palace. Their barracks face the palace across the square.

The square is connected to the lower-level town via the red brick-paved Rampe Major and its two gates, all dating from the 16th century, which until the 19th century were the only means of approach from Condamine. ⚫ Bus: 1, 2 to Monaco Ville

CULTURE

L'Historial des Princes de Monaco (Musée de Cires) (Historical Waxworks Museum)
The history of the Grimaldi princes is presented in tableaux of life-size wax figures, many clothed in authentic costumes. ⚫ 27 rue Basse ⚫ 93 30 39 05 ⚫ 10.00–18.00 Mar–Sept; 11.00–17.00 Oct–Feb ⚫ Bus: 1, 2 to Monaco Ville. Admission charge

Musée de la Chapelle de la Visitation
The 17th-century baroque Chapelle de la Visitation, a short walk north from the Oceanographic Institute, houses a remarkable, privately assembled collection of religious art, including works by Rubens and Italian masters of the baroque period. ⚫ pl. de la Visitation ⚫ 93 50 07 00 ⚫ 10.00–16.00 Tues–Sun ⚫ Bus: 1, 2 to Monaco Ville. Admission charge

Musée des Souvenirs Napoléoniens & Archives Historiques du Palais (Museum of Napoleon Souvenirs and Historic Archives of the Palace)
Two museums in one, housed in the south wing of the Palais Princier.

The ground floor is the Napoleonic Museum, with a collection of more than 1,000 objects and documents relating to, or once owned by, the Emperor Napoleon I. Considering Napoleon's rough treatment of the House of Grimaldi (see page 14), it seems quite generous of them to make space in their home for what is one of the finest collections of Napoleonic memorabilia in Europe.

The first floor of the wing is dedicated to the history of the Principality. Exhibits include the medieval Charter of Independence of Monaco, signed by King Louis XII of France, a letter written by Louis XIV to Prince Antoine I, uniforms of the Prince's Guards, and medals bestowed by and upon the Princes of Monaco. ⓐ pl. du Palais ⓣ 93 25 18 31 Ⓦ www.palais.mc Ⓛ 09.30–18.00 June–Sept; 10.00–17.00 Oct–mid-Nov; 10.30–12.00, 14.00–16.30 Tues–Sun, mid-Dec–May. Closed, 25 Dec and 1 Jan Ⓝ Bus: 1, 2 to Monaco Ville. Admission charge

Musée Océanographique (Oceanographic Institute Museum)

Perched on a cliff overlooking the sea, the Oceanographic Institute is a world-class museum and a fascinating excursion for both adults and children. Born out of the passion held by two of Monaco's former princes for the sea, the museum has grown into an impressive collection of rare marine specimens and antique sea exploration devices.

On the top floor you can have lunch in the La Terrasse café while admiring the magnificent views of Monaco and the Italian Riviera, and there is also a good museum shop.

Once you've visited the museum (a full visit should take about an hour and a half), consider taking the quaint touristic train (see page 81) that stops outside the museum for a guided tour back down into Monte Carlo. ⓐ av. St-Martin ⓣ 93 15 36 00 Ⓦ www.oceano.mc

Ⓞ *What better setting for a marine research institute?*

🕒 09.30–19.00 Apr–June, Sept; 09.30–19.30 July–Aug; 10.00–18.00
Oct–Mar ⓝ Bus: 1, 2 to Monaco Ville. Admission charge

RETAIL THERAPY

There are literally dozens of souvenir and gift shops squeezed
into the narrow streets of Monaco-Ville. They all offer similar wares,
including handicrafts and fun jewellery, and it pays to browse before
buying, as the further away from the tourist epicentres (especially
in the Palais Princier) you stroll, the more affordable the prices are
likely to be. Perhaps the best places to find authentic Monégasque
handicrafts and products are the Boutique du Rocher and Ombre
& Soleil. If you want merchandise relating to the Grand Prix, then
make for Shopping F1, just off the place du Palais.

Boutique du Rocher ⓐ 11 rue Emile de Loth ⓣ 93 30 33 99
🕒 10.30–18.00

Ombre & Soleil ⓐ 29 rue Comte Felix Gastaldi ⓣ 93 50 07 15
🕒 09.30–19.30

Shopping F1 ⓐ 8 rue Basse ⓣ 93 30 84 50 🕒 09.30–20.00

TAKING A BREAK

Le Castelroc £ ❶ A traditional café/restaurant in a prime position;
the prices make this clear, but it's very convenient for a coffee break
or lunch after visiting the Palace. Local dishes are a speciality – try
a traditional *barbajuan* (see page 28). ⓐ pl. du Palais ⓣ 93 30 36 68
🕒 09.00–17.00 ⓝ Bus: 1, 2 to Monaco Ville

Crêperie du Rocher £ ❷ There's nothing better for a light lunch than a savoury pancake or a pizza, and this *crêperie* on a side street off the palace square specialises in both. ❸ 12 rue Comte Felix Gastaldi ☎ 93 30 09 64 🕐 11.30–23.00 🚌 Bus: 1, 2 to Monaco Ville

Terrasse du Musée £ ❸ The café at the top of the Oceanographic Institute (see page 84) is a great place to enjoy sea views and a drink or spot of lunch. ❸ av. St-Martin 🕐 As for the museum 🚌 Bus: 1, 2 to Monaco Ville

Chocolaterie de Monaco ££ ❹ Enjoy tea fit for a king – or a prince – at this tea room, home of the prince's official chocolate suppliers. ❸ pl. de la Visitation ☎ 97 97 88 88 🚌 Bus: 1, 2 to Monaco Ville

AFTER DARK

Monaco-Ville is a district of small, generally family-run restaurants, but only a limited number stay open in the evenings.

RESTAURANTS

Pasta Roca £ ❺ A good selection of pizzas and local and regional specialities. ❸ 23 rue Comte Felix Gastaldi ☎ 93 30 44 22 🕐 11.00–15.00, 19.00–22.30 🚌 Bus: 1, 2 to Monaco Ville

Saint-Nicolas £ ❻ The quiet location near the cathedral and a good selection of traditional Monégasque and Provençal dishes make this a popular choice, daytime or evening. ❸ 6 rue de l'Église ☎ 93 30 30 41 🕐 12.00–15.00, 19.00–22.30 🚌 Bus: 1, 2 to Monaco Ville

Le Pinocchio £–££ ❼ This traditional Italian restaurant is just off the Palace Square. ⓐ rue Comte Felix Gastaldi ❶ 93 30 96 20 ⓛ 12.00–15.00, 19.00–23.00 ⓝ Bus: 1, 2 to Monaco Ville

U Cavagnetu £–££ ❽ Excellent seafood and local dishes at this traditional establishment with a large dining terrace and a cosy interior. ⓐ 14–16 rue Comte Felix Gastaldi ❶ 93 30 35 80 ⓛ 12.00–15.00, 19.00–23.00 ⓝ Bus: 1, 2 to Monaco Ville

ENTERTAINMENT

With all the nightlife of Monte Carlo only a few hundred metres away, not many visitors or locals choose to make Monaco-Ville their night-time destination. However, it does possess two attractions, both open-air and summer only, and both near the tip of the promontory: the Cinéma d'Eté on top of the Pêcheurs car park (see page 31), and the Théâtre de Fort Antoine, a converted 18th-century fortress which holds up to 350 spectators in a tiered semi-circle, providing a magical setting for drama and music events.

Théâtre de Fort Antoine ⓐ av. de la Quarantaine ❶ 93 15 80 00

● *Monaco-Ville is the city's best area for traditional bistros*

La Condamine & Moneghetti

La Condamine, once the vegetable gardens of the Prince's castle, is the most bustling and down-to-earth area of Monaco, a district of busy shopping streets and small hotels hemmed in between the main railway line and the harbour. Moneghetti, beyond the railway and backing onto the mountains, is quieter, but has one or two worthwhile attractions.

SIGHTS & ATTRACTIONS

Église Ste-Dévote (St Dévote's Church)

This 19th-century chapel replaced a medieval oratory built on the spot where a ship carrying the remains of St Dévote, a Corsican martyr, supposedly ran aground after a storm in the 4th century AD. She became the patron saint of Monaco. According to another legend a thief tried to make off with her relics when they turned out to have miraculous powers, but he was caught by local fishermen, who burnt his boat. At dusk on 26 January, the eve of the saint's day, a boat is burnt in commemoration, following a torchlight procession to the chapel. ⓐ pl. Ste-Dévote ⓣ 93 50 25 60 ⓛ Daily ⓝ Bus: 1, 2, 5, 6 to Place Ste Dévote

Jardin Exotique, La Grotte de l'Observatoire and Le Musée d'Anthropologie Préhistorique

Jardin Exotique (Exotic Garden) One of Monaco's most popular attractions is this dry garden, created on a rock face in Moneghetti in 1933 and containing thousands of weird and wonderful cacti and other succulents from all over the world, which thrive in the area's microclimate. It is more colourful than it sounds, since many of

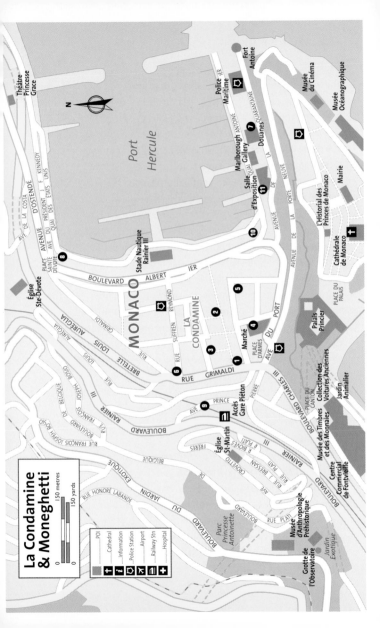

La Condamine & Moneghetti

0   150 metres
0   150 yards

POI
Cathedral
Information
Police Station
Airport
Railway Stn
Hospital

Port Hercule

MONACO

LA CONDAMINE

Théâtre Princesse Grace
Église Ste-Dévote
AVE DE LA COSTA
AVENUE D'OSTENDE
AVENUE DU PRESIDENT F KENNEDY
AVE DU QUAI DES ETATS UNIS
PLACE SAINTE DEVOTE
BOULEVARD ALBERT 1ER
Stade Nautique Rainier III
RUE GRIMALDI
RUE AURECLIA
RUE LOUIS AURECLIA
RUE BRETELLE LOUIS
RUE SUFFREN REYMOND
RUE GRIMALDI
Marché
PLACE D'ARMES
AVE DU PORT
Palais Princier
PLACE DU PALAIS
Collection des Voitures Anciennes
Jardin Animalier
BOULEVARD CHARLES III
Musée des Timbres et des Monnaies
PLACE DU CANTON
Accès Gare Piéton
AVE PRINCE PIERRE
BOULEVARD RAINIER III
RUE CROUETTO
RUE J BRESSAN
RUE PLATI
AVE DES FRÈRES
Église St-Martin
RUE BIOVES
AVE CROVETTO
RUE PLATI
BOULEVARD DE BELGIQUE
RUE FRANÇOIS JOSEPH BOSIO
RUE LOUIS
BOULEVARD JOSEPH JOSEPH
RUE HONORÉ LABANDE
RUE DE BELGIQUE
BOULEVARD DU JARDIN EXOTIQUE
Parc Princesse Antoinette
Musée d'Anthropologie Préhistorique
Centre Commercial de Fontvieille
BOULEVARD
Grotte de l'Observatoire
Jardin Exotique
Mairie
L'Historial des Princes de Monaco
Cathédrale de Monaco
AVENUE DE LA PORTE NEUVE
Fort Antoine
Police Maritime
QUAI ANTOINE 1ER
Marlborough Gallery
Salle d'Exposition
Douanes
LA QUARANTAINE
Musée du Cinéma
Musée Océanographique
AVENUE DE LA PORTE NEUVE

N

① ② ③ ④ ⑤ ⑥ ⑦ ⑧ ⑨ ⑩

these plants have impressive blooms that flower at different times, creating year-round interest. The garden is an important international centre for the study and propagation of these plants. There is also a snack bar and a shop selling plants.

Grotte de l'Observatoire (Observatory Cave) Part of the same complex as the Jardin Exotique, the name of this attraction is slightly misleading, as it has nothing to do with stargazing. Opened to the public in 1950, it is a natural cavern, some 60 m (200 ft) below the Jardin Exotique, once occupied by Stone Age man and now filled with impressive stalagmites and stalactites. The full tour is a good two hours.

Musée d'Anthropologie Préhistorique (Museum of Prehistoric Anthropology) The Riviera region was a favourite dwelling site for prehistoric man, as evidenced in the nearby cave. This interesting museum displays the remains of mankind's occupation over the last million years, including exhibits ranging from Australopithecus to Homo sapiens in the human race and many extinct animals. ⓐ 62 blvd du Jardin Exotique ⓣ 93 15 29 80 ⓦ www.jardin-exotique.mc ⓛ 09.00–19.00 mid May–mid Sept; 09.00–18.00 or nightfall, mid-Sept–mid-May. Closed 19 Nov and 25 Dec ⓝ Bus: 2 to Jardin Exotique (the terminus for this route). One admission charge covers the garden, cave and museum.

Marlborough Gallery

Founded in London in 1946, the commercial Marlborough Gallery opened its Monaco outpost in 2000 in a converted warehouse near the port. As well as staging an ever-changing series of exhibitions of the contemporary and modern classic artists, it also represents some of the best-known names in modern art. ⓐ 4 quai Antoine 1er ⓣ 97 70 25 50 ⓦ www.marlborough-monaco.com ⓛ 10.00–18.00 Mon–Fri ⓝ Bus: 1, 2 to Princesse Stéphanie

Parc Princesse Antoinette

This delightful open space was purchased in 1916 by Prince Albert I, who was concerned to preserve the last remaining natural areas of his Principality from development. It was, and still is, an olive grove. There were 156 trees left at the time of purchase, to which the late Prince Rainier and his son Albert added a 157th in 1993 to commemorate Monaco joining the United Nations. As well as olive trees, the park contains flowerbeds and streams crossed by little bridges, making it a welcome refuge from the urban side of Monaco. Under Prince Louis II in the 1920s, the park was dedicated to the children of Monaco, and was named after his daughter Antoinette. It is now a multi-level supervised playground, with a mini Formula 1 circuit; open to two–ten-year-olds. The park is traditionally visited once a year on the last Sunday of June by the reigning monarch and most of the Monégasque population for a giant family picnic. ❸ 54 bis blvd du Jardin Exotique ❶ 93 30 92 12 ❹ 08.30–19.00 May–Sept, 08.30–18.00 Mar–Apr & Oct, 08.30–17.30 Nov–Feb ❷ Bus: 2 to Hector Otto. Admission to park free; small admission charge to playground

Place d'Armes

One side of this large square is dominated by the Condamine fruit and vegetable market. Sitting under the Rocher (or Rock) of Monaco, it is a natural meeting place for citizens and tourists, with plenty of pavement cafés, newsstands and other everyday conveniences. There's also a children's play area. ❷ Bus: 1, 2, 5, 6 to Place d'Armes

Port Hercule

The main harbour, also known as Port de Monaco, is where you'll find Monaco's most luxurious yachts, a succession of cruise ships and Monaco's newest project – the Digue, a floating jetty under construction. The centre of the quayside is dominated by the Olympic-sized swimming pool at the Stade Nautique Rainier III (see page 99), which is transformed into an ice rink during the winter months. The Port is also known for its themed fairs, notably its annual Christmas Village. Ⓝ Bus: 1, 2, 5, 6 to Princesse Stéphanie

RETAIL THERAPY

If you're shopping for everyday items, or looking for gifts and fashion items that bit more affordable than what Monte Carlo has to offer, make for La Condamine. For anything nautical, head for the quaysides of Port Hercule and their surrounding streets. For produce and a cheerful market atmosphere, choose the big central market. For all other shopping, you need look no further than the rue Princesse Caroline, the nearby rue Grimaldi and behind it the rue de la Turbie.

Le Marché de la Condamine, Monaco's main market, has plenty to offer, in spite of the rather functional appearance of the building itself. The exterior is dominated by a flower market; inside you'll find many food stalls – bakers, butchers, *charcutiers* – offering Monégasque specialities. If you're planning a picnic, this should be your first stop. It's also a social centre, with a couple of welcoming and agreeable bars, and is the best place to observe the everyday life of Monaco away from the glitz and millionaire ambience. ⓐ pl. d'Armes Ⓝ Bus: 1, 2, 5, 6 to Place d'Armes

▶ *Le Marché de la Condamine spills out into the place d'Armes*

TAKING A BREAK

Bar de Monaco £ ❶ The name suggests that the whole Principality heads to this busy marketplace bar, and sometimes that seems not far short of the truth. Lots of local life. ⓐ 1 pl. d'Armes ❶ 93 30 12 58 ● 07.00–20.00 ⓝ Bus: 1, 2, 5, 6 to Place d'Armes

Le Condamine £ ❷ Take a break from shopping at this all-day café, ideally situated in the middle of Monaco's premier shopping street. ⓐ 16 rue Princesse Caroline ❶ 93 30 17 83 ● 07.00–24.00 (23.00 in winter) ⓝ Bus: 1, 2, 5, 6 to Place d'Armes

Le Huit et demi £–££ ❸ An excellent and terribly popular eatery, the 8 et demi enjoys a loyal fanbase. The cooking is typical of what you would expect (and hope) to find in a French bistro: well-prepared and flavourful fare, containing plenty of fresh ingredients from the day's market. ⓐ 4 rue Langlé ❶ 93 50 97 02 ● 12.00–23.00 ⓝ Bus: 1, 2, 5, 6 to Place d'Armes

Le Zinc £–££ ❹ This busy bar in the heart of the covered market has bags of atmosphere and is one place where you can be sure of mixing with the locals. ⓐ Marché de la Condamine, pl. d'Armes ❶ 93 50 93 99 ● 05.30–13.30 Mon–Sat ⓝ Bus: 1, 2, 5, 6 to Place d'Armes

AFTER DARK

RESTAURANTS
Royal Thai £ ❺ Satisfying spicy dishes, including some great vegetarian treats – unusual for meat-loving Monaco. Great for lunch or dinner.

● *Port Hercule bustles with life as night falls*

@ 18 rue de Millo ● 93 30 16 14 ● 97 98 10 94 ● 12.00–14.00, 19.00–22.30 ● Buses: 1, 2, 5, 6 to Stade Nautique

Monkey's £–££ ● This busy bar and restaurant is always teeming with local twentysomethings. The menu is a good mix of fun and sophisticated and there's a great, very reasonable lunchtime menu. @ 1 rue Princesse Florestine ● 93 25 60 30 ● 12.00–01.00 Mon–Sat ● Bus: 1, 2, 5, 6 to Place d'Armes

Stars'N'Bars £–££ ● This three-storey bar, restaurant and entertainment complex overlooking the harbour (and the paddocks of the Grand Prix championship) is as much a favourite with tourists as with celebrity customers, who include some of the best known names in Formula 1 racing. Food style is predominantly American and Tex-Mex. Among its other attractions are a cybercafé, a kids' room and an upstairs club with live bands. @ 6 quai Antoine 1er

📞 97 97 95 95 🌐 www.starsnbars.com 🕐 11.00–24.00 Mon–Thur, 11.00–02.00 Fri–Sun 🚌 Bus: 1, 2, 5, 6 to Place d'Armes

Tender to... £–££ ❽ This brand new restaurant replaced the much-loved Restaurant du Port but is already proving a hit with its modern takes on classic Mediterranean dishes. 📍 quai Albert 1er 📞 93 50 77 21 🕐 12.00–15.00, 19.00–23.00 🚌 Bus: 1, 2, 5, 6 to Place Ste Dévote

Vecchia Firenze £–££ ❾ A good place to head for lunch or dinner if you happen to be near the station, where the choice otherwise isn't great. Solid menu of pasta, pizza and other Italian-Mediterranean fare. 📍 Hotel Versailles, 4 av. Prince Pierre 📞 93 30 27 70 🕐 12.00–14.00, 19.00–22.30 Tues–Sun 🚌 Bus: 1, 2, 5, 6 to Place d'Armes

Café Grand Prix ££ ❿ Well-presented brasserie food and a harbour view, plus a bar with music that doesn't close till well into the morning. 📍 quai Antoine 1er 📞 93 25 56 90 🕐 Restaurant: 12.00–14.30, 19.45–22.30 Tues–Sat. Bar: 10.30–05.00 Mon–Fri, 19.00–05.00 Sat & Sun. Both closed in Feb 🚌 Bus: 1, 2, 5, 6 to Place d'Armes

Quai des Artistes ££ ⓫ This chic Parisian-style bistro is one of the top places for seafood and boasts a lively atmosphere. 📍 4 quai Antoine 1er 📞 97 97 97 77 🕐 12.30–14.30, 19.30–23.15 🚌 Bus: 1, 2, 5, 6 to Place d'Armes

ENTERTAINMENT

As well as Stars'N'Bars and Café Grand Prix, a lively late-night bar is:
Slammers A popular candle-lit hangout with two-for-one drinks during happy hour (17.00–20.00). 📍 6 rue Suffren Reymond 📞 97 70 36 56 🕐 17.00–01.00 🚌 Bus: 1, 2, 5, 6 to Stade Nautique

ACTIVITIES & RELAXATION

Christmas Village

Every year from the beginning of December, the quay overlooking the port is transformed into a winter wonderland complete with tiny chalets, activities for young and old, entertainers, and oyster and champagne stands – and a different theme each year. The success of the Christmas Village is paving the way for additional events throughout the year, so watch this space. ⓐ quai Albert 1er ⓣ 93 15 28 63 (Mairie) Ⓝ Bus: 1, 2, 5, 6 to Stade Nautique

Stade Nautique Rainier III

There's no need to go out to the beach at Larvotto if you fancy a swim. This watersports stadium, with an open-air Olympic-size swimming pool, sits in the very middle of Monaco, perched over the harbour, with great views of the town and the mountains as a bonus. The 1,250 sq m (12,000 sq ft) pool is filled with 3,000 cu m (100,000 cu ft) of treated seawater kept at 26°C (79°F). You can pay as you go in or buy books of tickets (carnets) for repeat visits, and mats and parasols can be hired. From December to March it serves instead as Monaco's ice rink. ⓐ quai Albert 1er ⓣ 93 30 64 83 ⓛ 09.00–20.00 Tues–Sun, 09.00–18.00 Mon, June–mid Sept; 09.00–18.00 May & mid-Sept–mid-Oct Ⓝ Bus: 1, 2, 5, 6 to Stade Nautique. Admission charge

◗ *Brightly-coloured boats adorn the coasts of the area*

Fontvieille

Although Fontvieille is mainly residential, it contains a surprising number of museums, many of them clustered conveniently near the edge of the old town, as well as stadia, a sculpture trail and one of Monaco's most beautiful gardens. The district is walkable and very accessible from other parts of Monaco: bus routes 5 and 6 both connect Fontvieille with the central rail station, La Condamine and Monaco-Ville, and bus 6 also runs through Monte Carlo via the Casino.

SIGHTS & ATTRACTIONS

Helicopter trips

Fontvieille is the site of Monaco's heliport and, as well as operating the scheduled heli-taxi service to and from Nice Airport (see page 50), two helicopter companies offer a range of trips over the surrounding area, some of them combined with other pusuits such as golf, skiing and haute cuisine – even weddings. Typically a trip around Monaco will take 10–15 minutes, one taking in most of the Riviera 40–60 minutes. Fares start at €50 per person, with a minimum of four passengers. **Héli Air Monaco** ⓐ Héliport de Monaco, av. des Ligures ⓣ 92 05 00 50 ⓦ www.heliairmonaco.com ⓝ Bus: 5, 6 to Héliport

Jardin Animalier (Zoo)

Close to the terrasses de Fontvieille is Monaco's zoological garden, opened by the late Prince Rainier in 1954. Overlooking the Fontvieille harbour from the southern side of the Rock of Monaco-Ville, this must be one of the best-sited zoos in the world. Although it's not large, it houses over 50 species of exotic birds and animals, including

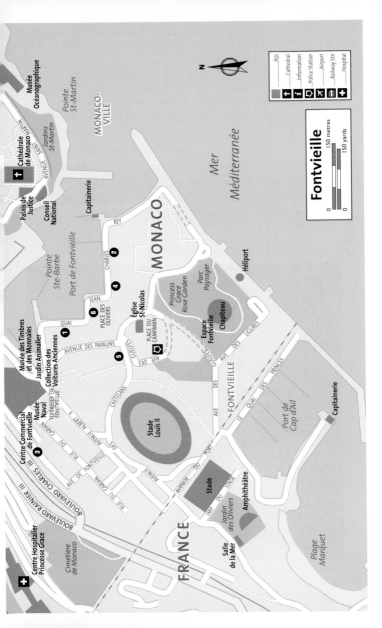

black panthers, white tigers and hippopotami, as well as lemurs, racoons and a wide range of reptiles. Because of pressure on space, some of its larger inhabitants, including large primates and the former star resident, Margareth the white rhino, have had to be transferred to other zoos in recent years; nevertheless, this collection of birds and beasts is well cared-for and certain to appeal to younger visitors. ⓐ 9 terrasses de Fontvieille/espl. Rainier III ⓣ 93 50 40 30 ⓛ 09.00–12.00, 14.00–19.00 June–Sept; 10.00–12.00, 14.00–18.00 Mar–May; 10.00–12.00, 14.00–17.00 Oct–Feb

● *The Scupture Trail ends in the well kept Parc Paysager de Fontvieille*

Bus: 1, 2, 5, 6 to Place d'Armes. Admission charge

Parc Paysager de Fontvieille & Chemin des Sculptures

In the heart of Fontvieille, off the avenue des Papalins, lies this pleasant 4-hectare (10-acre) landscaped park, laid out with an impressive collection of trees and shrubs from all over the world and a small lake, populated by ducks and swans, in the middle. The nearby Chemin des Sculptures or Sculpture Trail shows off a large number of the 100 or so modern sculptures that decorate the streets throughout Monaco (see page 46). In the middle of the park is the Espace Fontvieille, a large arena that is used to stage many shows and exhibitions, the most notable of which is the annual International Circus Festival in January. ⓐ av. des Papalins ⓛ sunrise–sunset Ⓝ Bus: 5, 6 to Roseraie

○ *Monaco's best-loved Princess is commemorated in the rose garden that bears her name*

Princess Grace Rose Garden

Follow the sculpture trail and you will come to the Princess Grace Rose Garden, on a slight slope inland from the Fontvieille Park. The much-loved wife of Rainier III met her tragic death in a car accident in 1982; two years later, the Prince inaugurated this garden in her memory. Over 4,000 bushes, representing 150 varieties of rose, are planted here and their combined fragrance is overwhelming. ⓐ Next to Fontvieille Park ⓒ sunrise–sunset ⓝ Bus: 5, 6 to Roseraie

Stade Louis II

This gigantic concrete stadium is no asset to Monaco visually, but it does provide the Principality with an Olympic-standard sports complex, including gymnasia, a running track and an indoor pool, and the home ground of Monaco's high-flying football team, AS Monaco. It's possible to take a one-hour guided tour with a commentary in English. ⓐ 7 av. des Castelans ⓣ 92 05 40 11 ⓒ Tours at 09.30, 11.00, 14.30 and 16.00 Mon, Tues, Thur & Fri ⓝ Bus: 5, 6 to Stade Louis II. Admission charge

● *Stade Louis II, seaside home of AS Monaco*

Terrasses de Fontvieille

This terrace, overlooking the Port de Fontvieille (the smaller of Monaco's two ports), is easily reached on foot from the place du Palais. It is the home of Fontvieille's three museums (see below), which are among Monaco's best, and the zoo. 🚌 Bus: 1, 2, 5, 6 to Place d'Armes

CULTURE

Three diverse collections occupy much of the terrasses de Fontvieille, the closest part of the district to the old town.

Collection des Voitures Anciennes (Classic Car Exhibition)

This is the private collection of the late Prince Rainier III, who was an avid motor-sport enthusiast and collector of cars that appealed to him, not just luxury or sports cars. From the 1903 De Dion Bouton to the legendary 1986 Lamborghini Countach, the perfectly maintained exhibits constitute a virtual history of 20th-century automobiles. 🅐 terrasses de Fontvieille 🕐 92 05 28 56 🕓 Daily, except 25 Dec, 10.00–18.00 🚌 Bus: 1, 2, 5, 6 to Place d'Armes. Admission charge

Musée des Timbres et des Monnaies (Stamps and Coins Museum)

One of Monaco's traditional official sources of revenue, apart from the earnings of the Casino and associated hotels, has been the issue of postage stamps. Long before most other countries realised the financial potential of philately, Monaco was regularly issuing collectible editions of stamps, distinguished by the quality of their artwork. The country began issuing its own coinage in 1640 and many of its coins are prized by collectors. This specialist museum commemorates the history of Monégasque stamps and coins with a well-presented exhibition displaying both the artefacts themselves and the changing technology used to make them. The Principality's historic output can be viewed in the new multimedia centre. Every paying visitor gets to take away a Monaco stamp. ⓐ 11 terrasses de Fontvieille ⓣ 93 15 41 50 ⓛ 10.00–18.00 July–Sept; 10.00–17.00 Oct–June ⓝ Bus: 1, 2, 5, 6 to Place d'Armes. Admission charge

Musée Naval (Maritime Museum)

Further along the terrasses is this collection of scale models of famous ships, some 250 in all. Monaco has a long history of seafaring, from the Middle Ages (its small navy served the French kings against the English in the Hundred Years War) to the 20th century, when Prince Albert I sent scientific expeditions across the globe. Even if your interest in the subject is slight, you can't fail to be impressed by the detail and size of the models (for instance, that of the *Titanic* is over 3 m/10 ft long); if you are into maritime history, or your kids are, you may find yourself spending several hours here. ⓐ 1 terrasses de Fontvieille ⓣ 92 05 28 48 ⓦ www.musee-naval.mc ⓛ 10.00–18.00 ⓝ Bus: 1, 2, 5, 6 to Place d'Armes. Admission charge

RETAIL THERAPY

The district's shopping is dominated by the large Centre Commercial de Fontvieille, which sits squarely at the junction of Fontvieille and Monaco-Ville. Its large Carrefour hypermarket meets most of the needs of this residential district (and is very useful for virtually anything a visitor might need, from take-away food to cheap clothing). There are many smaller specialist shops within the Centre, too. Add to that plenty of bars and cafés for R&R and you might find

it a welcome contrast to the price tags (or lack of them) in the
Monte Carlo boutiques.

TAKING A BREAK

The bars and cafés of Fontvieille cluster, naturally enough, on quai
Jean-Charles Rey, the southwest side of the Port de Fontvieille, from
where you can look across the luxury yachts to the impressive side
of the Rocher de Monaco. The other good place for a quick lunchtime
bite is the Centre Commercial de Fontvieille, which has a McDonald's
and several brasseries/pizzerias.

Gerhard's Café £ ❶ If only a good German-style beer will quench your
thirst, you can't get better than the Fürstenberg at this portside bar.
🅐 42 quai Jean-Charles Rey 🕿 92 05 25 79 🕒 08.00–01.00 Mon–Sat,
18.00–01.00 Sun 🚌 Bus: 5, 6 to Port de Fontvieille

Ship & Castle £ ❷ For those who prefer a pub atmosphere, this
would-be piece of Old England is next door to Gerhard's. 🅐 42 quai
Jean-Charles Rey 🕿 92 05 76 72 🕒 11.00–02.00 Mon–Fri, 11.00–03.00
Sat & Sun 🚌 Bus: 5, 6 to Port de Fontvieille

ZenZen £ ❸ Newcomer ZenZen offers healthy Asian tapas in an
upmarket fast-food setting with an emphasis on ethics and fair trade.
🅐 Centre Commercial de Fontvieille 🕿 97 77 03 33 🕒 07.00–22.00
Mon–Sat 🚌 Bus: 5, 6 to Port de Fontvieille

AFTER DARK

RESTAURANTS

L'Eden Bleu £ ❹ Friendly quayside brasserie with an amazing number of ways of serving *moules frites*. ⓐ 32 quai Jean-Charles Rey ❶ 99 99 99 69 ❷ 17.00–01.00 Mon–Sat, 12.00–15.00 Sun Ⓝ Bus: 5, 6 to Port de Fontvieille

La Brasserie £–££ ❺ This exceptional restaurant follows the same high standards as the hotel in which it is housed. ⓐ Hotel Columbus, 23 av. des Papalins ❶ 92 05 90 00 ❷ 12.00–22.30 Ⓝ Bus: 5, 6 to Port de Fontvieille

Beef Bar & Capitano ££ ❻ Immensely popular Italian-run restaurant specialising in high-quality cuts of beef and fish. Booking is essential. ⓐ 42 quai Jean-Charles Rey ❶ 97 77 09 29 ❷ 12.00–15.00 Mon–Sat, 19.30–24.00 Ⓝ Bus: 5, 6 to Port de Fontvieille

ENTERTAINMENT

Espace Polyvalent Salle du Canton This entertainment venue near the Centre Commercial has a varied programme of concerts, opera and theatre, as well as discos and music festivals throughout the year. It's worth checking the current programme with the tourist office or via the website. ⓐ terrasses de Fontvieille, 25–29 av. Prince Héréditaire Albert ❶ 93 10 12 10 Ⓦ www.monaco-spectacle.com for programme and online booking; www.monaco-mairie.mc for general information Ⓝ Bus: 1, 2, 5, 6 to Place d'Armes

---

▶ *Picturesque Roquebrune is perched high above the eastern Riviera*

OUT OF TOWN
trips

Roquebrune & Menton

At one time, the Grimaldis of Monaco also ruled the neighbouring territories of Roquebrune and Menton to the northeast. By the mid-19th century both had been lost, albeit peacefully, to France. The proximity of these two French Riviera resorts makes them ideal destinations for a day (or even a half-day) out from Monaco. It would be possible to visit both in the same day, but to do them justice, allot a day each. Roquebrune Cap-Martin combines the picturesque attractions of an ancient hilltop village with the possibility of easy coastal walks round the Cap-Martin peninsula to the more modern resort area of Carnolés. Menton is a pretty old port town that is as much Italian as French and can claim to be the garden capital of the Riviera.

GETTING THERE

Both places are easily accessible by train from Monaco's Gare SNCF: Roquebrune is only five minutes away, and Menton just a ten-minute journey. Trains are frequent – at least a dozen a day from early morning to mid-evening, and return trains leave Menton up till as late as midnight. If you arrive at Roquebrune by rail, you'll have to climb a stepped path from the station up to the village, or take a taxi. Menton's Gare SNCF, however, is very central and a short, easy walk to the town centre and seafront.

If you're motoring, you can treat yourself to a drive along the winding Grande Corniche, or the slightly lower Moyenne Corniche, both of which have great views of the coast, for the passenger at least – the roads are famous for their hairpin corners. If you're not confident that you can take the corniches' bends, head out to the

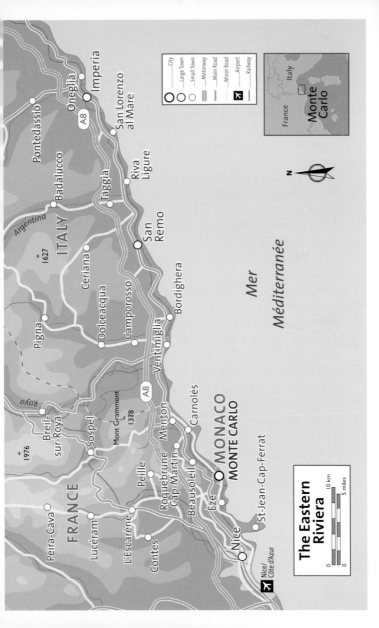

The Eastern Riviera

	Motorway	
○ City	Main Road	
○ Large Town	Minor Road	
○ Small Town	Railway	
	✈ Airport	

Monte Carlo

France · Italy

ITALY

Imperia
Oneglia
San Lorenzo al Mare
Pontedassio
Badalucco
Riva Ligure
Taggia
Argentina
San Remo
Ceriana
Bordighera
Dolceacqua
Camporosso
Pigna
Ventimiglia

1627

FRANCE

Breil-sur-Roya
Roya
Sospel
Mont Grammont 1378
Carnolés
Peïra-Cava
Peille
Menton
Lucéram
Roquebrune Cap-Martin
L'Escarène
Beausoleil
MONACO
MONTE CARLO
Contes
Èze
St-Jean-Cap-Ferrat
✈ Nice/Côte d'Azur
Nice

1976

Mer Méditerranée

N

0				10 km
0		5 miles		

A8 *autoroute* and take exit 58 to Roquebrune, exit 59 for Menton.
Roquebrune village is not suitable for motor traffic but there's
plenty of parking outside it.

ROQUEBRUNE CAP-MARTIN

SIGHTS & ATTRACTIONS

This beautifully preserved fortified village overlooks the Mediterranean
and the Cap-Martin peninsula. The maze of narrow streets was originally
intended to confuse any enemy that penetrated the outer defences, as
it does today's visitors – but it's too small to get seriously lost in. Just
outside the village on the chemin de Menton is what is reputed to be
the world's oldest olive tree. The other main attraction, other than the
atmosphere, is the Château at the top of the village, with four floors
of historical exhibits and a dungeon. Once a fortress of the Princes of
Monaco, it was designed to be garrisoned by no more than six men, and
the tour gives a fascinating insight into medieval military and daily life.

From the railway station you can walk the coastal path around
the foot of the Cap-Martin peninsula, and just round the bend of
the Baie de Roquebrune you'll come across Le Cabanon. Among the
many personalities who have chosen to live in this picturesque part
of the world was the architect Le Corbusier, and Le Cabanon was his
beach shack; open to visitors by arrangement. He had strong views
about the way the seaside was being developed, and Le Cabanon
represents his solution, a kind of modular seaside cabin. Le Corbusier
drowned while swimming in the bay in 1965, and his impressive,
self-designed memorial can be seen in Roquebrune's cemetery.

 You'll find plenty of cafés in the atmospheric streets of old Roquebrune

Tourist office This is actually in Carnolés, 2 km (1 mile) along the coast from Roquebrune village. ❸ 218 av. Aristide Briand, Carnolés ❶ 00 33 4 93 35 62 87 Ⓦ www.rocquebune-cap-martin.com

Château de Roquebrune ❸ pl. William Ingram, Roquebrune ❶ 04 93 35 07 22 Ⓛ 10.00–12.30, 15.00–19.30 July & Aug (afternoon opening is 14.00–18.30 in other months, but closing 17.00 in winter). Admission charge

Le Cabanon ❷ av. Le Corbusier Ⓛ Tues and Fri am visits are arranged by the tourist office and must be booked there. Admission charge

ACTIVITIES
Beaches You'll find two secluded beaches, Plage du Golfe Bleu and Plage du Buse, just below Roquebrune rail station.

Walking The tourist office has a good map of recommended walks around Roquebrune and the Cap-Martin peninsula.

CAFÉS, RESTAURANTS & ENTERTAINMENT
Roquebrune Cap-Martin is not famed for its nightlife (it could hardly compete with Monte Carlo on its doorstep), but the area is well provided with cafés and restaurants. Most of the pizzerias and budget eateries are in the built-up area of Carnolés, but there are still several options for a mid-morning or midday break in the old village itself: there are two restaurants for a leisurely lunch or atmospheric supper on the place des Deux Frères, a small square with great views across the bay to Monaco. Around the foot of Cap-Martin you'll find several delightful seaside restaurants and cafés, as well as some lovely beaches.

Fraises et Chocolat £ A *salon de thé* in the old village that serves luscious gâteaux, as its name suggests: good for a mid-morning snack or light lunch. ❷ 1 rue Raymond Poincaré, Roquebrune ❶ 00 33 6 67 08 32 20 ❸ 09.00–18.00 (21.00 in summer) Fri–Wed. Closed late Nov–early Dec and first week in Mar

La Grotte £ Grills and seafood are the specialities at this good-value café/restaurant in the village. ❷ pl. des Deux Frères, Roquebrune ❶ 00 33 4 93 28 99 00 ❸ 12.00–14.30, 19.00–22.00. Closed every Wed and most of Nov

Snack Bar Alaska £ This café is almost guaranteed to be open for some rest and recuperation at the end of your walk around the peninsula. ❷ av. Winston Churchill, Cap-Martin ❶ 00 33 4 93 41 33 76 ❸ 08.00–24.00 (21.00 in winter)

Les Deux Frères ££ Gastronomic dining at this hotel restaurant, in the heart of the old village, is enhanced by the superb views from the terrace. ❷ pl. des Deux Frères, Roquebrune ❶ 00 33 4 93 28 99 00 ❿ www.lesdeuxfreres.com ❸ 12.00–14.00, 19.30–22.00 (closed Mon & Tues lunchtime in summer, Sun & Mon evening in winter)

L'Hippocampe ££ A nice location for a leisurely lunch or early evening meal on the far side of Cap-Martin, looking out over the sea from its dining terrace, the 'Seahorse' specialises in seafood. Customers can also use its private beach. ❷ 44 av. Winston Churchill, Cap-Martin ❶ 00 33 4 93 35 81 91 ❸ 12.00–14.30, 19.30–21.30 Tues–Sun

ACCOMMODATION

There are at least 11 hotels in this area, all of them close enough to the rail stations of Roquebrune and Carnolés to make commuting into Monaco a viable alternative to staying in the Principality.

Le Roquebrune £ This *chambre d'hôtes* (B&B) has five rooms, all with showers. About 500 m from Roquebrune station, it's also convenient for the beaches and the village. ❷ 11 av. Jean Jaurès, Roquebrune ❶ 00 33 4 93 35 00 16 Ⓦ www.leRoquebrune.com

Hotel des Deux Frères £–££ The only hotel in the old village itself, beautifully situated. ❷ pl. des Deux Frères, Roquebrune ❶ 00 33 4 93 28 99 00 Ⓦ www.lesdeuxfreres.com

Hotel Alexandra ££ In an attractive location on the east side of the Cap-Martin peninsula, with views across the bay of Menton towards Italy, the Alexandra has 40 rooms all with private bath, and is open all year round. ❷ 93 av. Winston Churchill, Cap-Martin ❶ 00 33 4 93 35 65 45 Ⓦ www.hotel-alexandra.net

MENTON

SIGHTS & ATTRACTIONS

When you're in Menton you are nearly in Italy, and the town's architecture and pace of life confirms this. Until it broke free in 1848, Menton belonged to the Princes of Monaco, and it wasn't until 1860 that it voted to become part of France. The fact that it is also a prime retirement spot also adds to Menton's quiet, contented atmosphere.

▶ *Vieux Menton is the backdrop for the old harbour area*

During the late 19th and early 20th centuries Menton was a magnet for British and Russian aristocrats wintering on the Riviera, but many of the belle époque hotels in which they stayed have now vanished or have been turned into apartments. Though no longer the most fashionable resort on the Riviera, Menton still has a slightly refined air, but is certainly not stuffy. For a long time popular with well-to-do French and Italian holidaymakers, it now sees a growing number of visitors from overseas.

Its superb microclimate is what draws the retirees and it also makes Menton the lemon-growing capital of France, as well as guaranteeing the safety of the exotic shrubs that make its public and private gardens so attractive. On Shrove Tuesday you can have all the lemons you want with your pancakes – it's the day the town celebrates its principal crop with an exuberant Lemon Festival. If you're seriously interested in citrus fruits, then you should also make a beeline for La Citronneraie, a fragrant orchard that is Europe's leading collection of the plants of this species (the orchard is privately owned – access details from the tourist office).

The artist, writer and film director Jean Cocteau spent the last years of his life in Menton. Lasting memorials to him include the Salle des Mariages (wedding hall) of the town hall, which he decorated with vast, surreal frescoes, and the Musée Jean Cocteau, in a medieval bastion on the waterfront – the exhibits illustrate the versatility of his talents. Other notables who have lived and died in Menton, and are buried in the Cimetière du Vieux-Château high up in the town, include the British artist Aubrey Beardsley and William Webb Ellis, the inventor of rugby.

---

❿ *The architecture tells you that Menton was once part of Italy*

The modern centre of Menton is dominated by the twin avenues Verdun and Boyer, which are separated by the Jardins Biovès. At their southern end is Menton's Casino, which sits on the main seafront parade, the promenade du Soleil. Some of the best views of Menton are from the Vieux Port, the old harbour just east of the town centre. This area also offers a wide choice of cafés and bistros. The district behind the Vieux Port is the oldest part of town, the pedestrianised area known as Vieux Menton. Here you will find picture-postcard pretty Italianate buildings huddled around the baroque basilica of St-Michel and the Chapelle des Pénitents Blancs (the chapel of the medieval brotherhood of white-robed penitents).

Gardening enthusiasts will be pleased to hear that Menton is a premier *Ville Fleurie* of France and boasts the motto 'My City is a Garden'. Exotic gardens in or near the town include the Spanish-style Fontana Rosa, Le Val Rahmeh (tropical and subtropical plants, especially Solanaceae) and La Serre de la Madone (planted in the 1920s by Lawrence Johnston, creator of Britain's Hidcote Garden). The Giardini Botanici Hanbury (see page 127) are also accessible from the town. A full list of parks and gardens, all worth a visit, is obtainable at the tourist office.

There's usually an event taking place on the streets of Menton, in whichever month you visit. Apart from the 15-day Lemon Festival in February, the town hosts music festivals in May, July (including a Tango Festival, when the town takes on a South American theme) and August (with dancing in the streets during the 'Animations d'Eté'). June and September see special garden weeks, when private gardens are open. Children of all ages may prefer the Menton Grand Prix in August – it's for go-karts.

Fontana Rosa ⓐ av. Blasco Ibanez, about 2 km (1.5 miles) east of town
🕐 Guided visits 10.00 Fri Ⓝ Bus: 3 to Blasco Ibanez. Admission charge

Musée Jean Cocteau ⓐ Vieux Port ☎ 00 33 4 93 57 72 30
🕐 10.00–12.30, 14.00–18.00 Wed–Mon. Admission charge

Salle des Mariages ⓐ Mairie (Town Hall), pl. Ardoïno
☎ 00 33 4 92 10 50 00 🕐 08.30–12.30, 14.00–17.00 Mon–Fri
except public holidays. Admission charge

La Serre de la Madone ⓐ 74 route de Gorbio, about 3 km (2 miles) north
west of town ☎ 00 33 4 93 57 73 90 Ⓦ www.serredelamadone.com
🕐 10.00–18.00 Tues–Sun. Guided visits 15.00 Fri Ⓝ Bus: 7 to Val de
Gorbio. Admission charge

Tourist office ⓐ Palais de l'Europe, 8 av. Boyer ☎ 00 33 4 92 41 76 76
Ⓦ www.villedementon.com 🕐 09.00–19.00 (summer); 08.30–12.30,
13.30–18.00 Mon–Fri, 09.00–12.00, 14.00–18.00 Sat (winter)

Le Val Rahmeh ⓐ av. St-Jacques ☎ 00 33 4 93 35 86 72 🕐 10.00–12.30
Wed–Mon 15.00–18.00(summer), 14.00–17.00 (winter) Ⓝ Bus: 3
to Stade. Admission charge

RETAIL THERAPY

Menton attracts the sort of residents and visitors who can afford
luxury goods, and shops catering to their tastes congregate on the
av. Félix Faure and av. de Verdun in the middle of town. For smaller
specialist boutiques shops and the usual choice of gift shops,
head for Vieux Menton off the rue St-Michel.

Kalliste Buy handmade fragrances from this artisan parfumeur, including the local speciality *Eau de Menton*. ⓐ 1 rue de la Marne ❶ 00 33 4 93 41 45 87

Markets

Produce markets take place every morning in the covered market hall (ⓐ quai de Monléons) and at the Marché du Carie (ⓐ prom. Maréchal Leclerc), and there are *brocante* (bric-a-brac) markets on Fridays (ⓐ pl. aux Herbes) and on the second Sunday of each month (ⓐ espl. Palmero).

ACTIVITIES

Beaches After (or instead of) all that strenuous garden visiting, you may fancy a spot of swimming or sunbathing. Menton has well-kept, sandy beaches and the water quality has earned it an EU Blue Flag. Most of the beaches are private ones, attached to a café or restaurant, and charge an entrance fee, but the Plage des Sablettes is public and free.

Centre Nautique If you are interested in any of Menton's wide offering of watersports, this branch of the tourist office should be your first port of call for information on everything from surfboarding to kayaking. ⓐ prom. de la Mer ❶ 00 33 4 93 35 49 70

Centre Internationale de Plongée de la Maïna Menton's centre for diving and similar underwater activities. ⓐ 3 prom. de la Mer ❶ 00 33 4 93 41 66 41

Koaland Children's and family entertainment and activities, including mini-golf, go-karts, rides including a mini-roller coaster, bouncy castles and other diversions, about 1 km (0.5 miles) outside the town. ⓐ 5 av. de la Madone ⓣ 00 33 4 92 10 00 40 ⓛ 10.00–24.00 (19.00 in winter)

CAFÉS, RESTAURANTS & ENTERTAINMENT

Le Bristol £ Snack bar and *salon de thé* offering traditional rather than international fast food, including authentic *bruschetta*, excellent crêpes and ice creams. ⓐ 24 av. Carnot ⓣ 00 33 4 93 57 54 32 ⓛ Daily

Captain's Corner £ This portside bar and café offers great harbour views accompany a mid-morning coffee or a lunchtime drink. The menu is geared to seafood, as you would expect. In summer, expect to enjoy some entertainment from itinerant musicians. ⓐ quai Gordon Bennett (Vieux Port) ⓣ 00 33 4 92 41 04 25 ⓛ Daily

L'Albatros £–££ This charming bistro is unpretentious and typically Provençal, as is the food – not only fish dishes (including *bouillabaisse*) but also excellent beef and other meat cookery. ⓐ 31 quai Bonaparte ⓣ 00 33 4 93 35 94 64 ⓛ 12.00–15.00, 19.30–23.00 (22.00 in winter) Tues–Sun

Au Pistou £–££ Good seafood and local Mentonnais cuisine is offered at this harbourside restaurant. ⓐ quai Gordon Bennett (old port) ⓣ 00 33 4 93 57 45 89 ⓛ Daily

Rocamadour £–££ The owner of this restaurant, a Menton fixture for over a century, named it after his home town in Périgord, and echoes of the region on the menu include *foie gras* and *magret de canard* (duck breast). However, most of the cuisine is genuine Provençal. ⓐ 1 square Victoria ⓣ 00 33 4 93 35 76 04 ⓛ 12.00–14.30, 19.30–22.00 Thur–Tues

Casino Barrière de Menton More low-key than the casinos in Monte Carlo, this establishment offers roulette (French and English), blackjack and 150 slot machines. There's also a disco on Saturday evenings.
ⓐ av. Félix Faure ❶ 00 33 4 92 10 16 16 ❷ 10.00–03.00 (slots); 19.00–03.00 Mon–Thur, Sun, 19.00–04.00 Fri & Sat (gaming tables)

● *Flowery Menton revels in year-round sunshine*

ACCOMMODATION

There's plenty of accommodation in and around the town.
For an overview, visit ⓦ www.hotelmenton.com

Auberge de Jeunesse £ Menton's youth hostel makes up for the lack
of hostel facilities in Monaco itself. It's just above town, only a short
walk from centre. ⓐ plateau de St-Michel ⓣ 00 33 4 93 35 93 14

L'Aiglon £–££ A handsome white villa of the belle époque houses one
of the best hotels on this part of the Riviera. The décor is traditional
and it has a garden and pool. By the Parc de la Madone, about 1 km
(0.5 mile) from the centre. ⓐ 7 av. de la Madone ⓣ 00 33 4 93 57 55 55
ⓦ www.hotelaiglon.net

Le Globe £–££ This very centrally situated hotel is part of the ever-
reliable Logis de France association, guaranteeing good food and
an individual and authentically French ambience. ⓐ 21 av. de Verdun
ⓣ 00 33 4 92 10 59 70

Hôtel des Ambassadeurs ££–£££ Menton's grandest and most
luxurious hotel, built in 1865 and recently renovated, lies just off the
avenue Boyer in the centre. All the floors are dedicated to different
arts (music, literature, painting and cinema) and each suite is inspired
by a different artist or work. The hotel is completely non-smoking.
ⓐ 3 rue Partouneaux ⓣ 00 33 4 93 28 75 75
ⓦ www.ambassadeurs-menton.com

Ventimiglia & San Remo

As well as being a great base for visiting the French Riviera, Monaco is also a gateway to the other Riviera – the Ligurian one, just over the border in Italy. The resorts along this stretch of coastline are not as famous as their French counterparts, but the two most popular day-trip destinations, Ventimiglia and San Remo, are well worth a visit. Ventimiglia (usually spelt Vintimille on French maps) is only just over the Franco-Italian border, and San Remo, the biggest resort on the Ligurian Riviera, is just 35 km (20 miles) from Monaco.

GETTING THERE

The easiest way to reach either town is by train from Monaco's Gare SNCF. There are at least a dozen trains on weekdays and Saturdays, and only slightly fewer on Sundays, starting at around 06.00 until early evening. Check the timetables carefully at the station before deciding on your itinerary, and take note that there are a handful of express trains that require seat reservation in advance (but most of the departures around 08.00–09.00 don't). The last train back to Monaco from San Remo is around 23.00. Ventimiglia is a 22-minute journey and San Remo is just over an hour away.

If you're driving, simply join the A8 *autoroute* just outside Monaco follow the signs east for Menton and Italy. The border crossing is just past Menton and there are no formalities (but there may be customs checks in the opposite direction – see page 131); the motorway becomes the A10 in the Italian numbering system. Exits are well signposted. The journey times to both towns are similar to those of the trains, taking into account time taken from Monaco to the motorway and from the motorway to the town centres. There is also a winding coastal road that connects Monaco with both places via Menton, which will take you past the Giardini Hanbury (see page 130) – the views from it are great, but it will take you considerably longer.

VENTIMIGLIA

In the days before open frontiers in the EU, Ventimiglia's economy depended to a large extent on its position close to the border and the potential for duty-free shopping. Having lost that role to a great extent (though it still has a weekly market that attracts French and foreign visitors across the border), it has still a long way to go in developing the tourism potential of its position, climate and antiquity.

The town was old even before the Romans colonised it, calling it Albintimilium (from which comes its modern name, even though it

FLOWER POWER

The coastline from the French border to San Remo has been dubbed the Riviera dei Fiori (Coast of Flowers) by the Italians, and not without reason. Not only is it graced by some outstanding public gardens, such as the Giardini Botanici Hanbury at La Mortola (see page 130), but the climate makes this a prime spot for growing flowers as a crop. The canny Ligurians switched from lemon growing to floriculture in the early 1900s and today export blooms all over Europe. Devotees of the Viennese New Year's Day Concert, which is broadcast all over the world, will know that the stupendous floral arrangements that always decorate the concert hall are an annual gift from (and a superb advertisement for) the flower-growers of San Remo.

sounds like the Italian for 'twenty miles', and is even spelt 'XX miglia' on some maps). At the nearby Balzi Rossi ('Red Rocks') Prehistoric Museum you can still see the caves that were inhabited by *Homo erectus*, a predecessor of *Homo sapiens*.

The old walled medieval town, Ventimiglia Alta, sits on a steep hill apart from the modern centre. Its twisty streets and alleys are less restored and more medieval in atmosphere than those of Monaco-Ville or other Riviera towns, and are well worth exploring, and there are great mountain and sea views from the old walls. The old town has two particularly interesting churches. The Cathedral of the Assumption has a crypt dating from the 7th century that is probably part of an old Roman temple of the goddess Juno. The church of San Michele dates from the 10th century and will attract avid readers of *The Da Vinci Code*, as it has documented Templar connections and is one of the reputed hiding places of the Holy Grail, which may explain why it's always locked.

New Ventimiglia is mainly a day-trip shopping destination (see page 130–2). One of its most unusual features, which must be unique in this part of the world, is its total public ban on smoking. If you arrive in July or August you'll be able to enjoy the Battle of the Flowers (July) or the costumed parades and flag-waving of the Medieval August festival. The old town has a summer-long festival of pasta with street parties, the Sagra del Raviolo.

Tourist office IAT Ventimiglia ⓐ Via Cavour 61, Ventimiglia
ⓣ 00 39 01843 51183 ⓕ 00 39 01843 51183

SIGHTS & ATTRACTIONS
Balzi Rossi Prehistoric Museum ⓐ Grimaldi village, west of Ventimiglia
ⓣ 00 39 01843 8113 ⓒ 09.00–12.30, 14.00–18.00 Tues–Sun (summer); 09.00–13.00, 14.30–18.00 Tues–Sun (winter)

○ *Ventimiglia is less geared to tourism than its neighbours, which adds to its charm*

Giardini Botanici Hanbury (Gardens of the Villa Hanbury)

Just outside Ventimiglia, on the small promontory of La Mortola, is one of the world's most important, and most-visited, botanic gardens. English gardener and botanist Sir Thomas Hanbury, who had made a fortune as a trader in Shanghai, bought the site in 1867 and devoted the rest of his life to laying it out, not only as a garden in an idyllic setting but with the intention of creating an unparalleled collection of plants from all over the world that could thrive in the mild climate here. The care of the garden was taken over after World War I by his daughter-in-law Lady Dorothy Hanbury, and between the wars La Mortola was so famous that *The Times* of London would print a list of all the plants in flower there in their New Year's Day edition. Sadly, during World War II the garden found itself in a battle zone and ended up in ruins. It was sold to the Italian state in 1960 and after a long period of inadequate funding was given to the care of the University of Genoa, which, thanks in great part to the agitation of British garden enthusiasts, is now restoring it to its former glory.

Of its 18 hectares (44 acres), half are given over to native Ligurian plants and half to exotic specimens. Enthusiasts can follow a long path down to the coast and then uphill again, and marvel at the range of plants that will grow here. Highlights include an Australian forest, a Japanese garden and a collection of Far Eastern cycads.

ⓐ Corso Montecarlo 43, Cap Mortola, Ventimiglia ⓣ 00 39 0184 22 95 07 ⓦ www.amicihanbury.com ⓛ 10.00–17.00 May–mid-June, Oct; 10.00–16.00 Thur–Tues, Nov–Mar; 09.00–18.00 mid-June–Sept ⓝ Bus: 1 to La Mortola. Admission charge

RETAIL THERAPY

Apart from the lure of the 'designer' bargains in Ventimiglia market, the main shopping attractions of the Ligurian Riviera are culinary.

The region is famed for its gourmet food and drink, and high-quality olive oil, pesto, pasta and the local wines are all worth shopping for in the markets and shops of the two towns.

Ventimiglia new town still sticks to its pre-border shopping ethos; it has the highest concentration of liquor stores in Italy, and although there's now no duty-free logic to purchasing there, competition and the high volume of traffic keeps prices low. However, the main shopping draw is the Friday market on the seafront of the new town, attracting French residents and tourists with its cheap olive oil and other foodstuffs, and the wide range of 'designer' goods on sale. How do you know they're fakes? Just look at the prices.

BUYER BEWARE

Whatever your own views on the ethics of trading in goods that are imitations of the authentic branded items, you should be aware that buying as well as selling them is illegal in the EU. The Italian authorities have done little to control the trade in Ventimiglia market, apart from a very few high-profile arrests of traders (and some shoppers) for the benefit of the media. On the other hand, the French police and customs, with no vested interest in the continuation of the market, have been taking a tough line recently, stopping tourist cars at the border, confiscating contraband 'designer' merchandise and destroying it in front of the tearful purchasers (and the TV cameras). Whether this hard line will continue after its immediate publicity value fades remains to be seen, but before you hand over your cash for that bargain item, bear in mind that it may not make it past the border.

If you want to buy any of the very realistic imitations of brand-name bags, watches and fashions, get there early on Friday morning (the market starts at about 08.00 and goes on till 15.00 or later) and haggle like mad. If you pay more than 50 per cent of the initial asking price you've been duped. Be aware also that the trains to Ventimiglia are very crowded on Fridays, for obvious reasons, and if you're driving there you may have to park some way out of town.

CAFÉS, RESTAURANTS & ENTERTAINMENT

Liguria is the original home of pesto and focaccia, and is proud of its distinctive cuisine. It would be a pity not to sample some of it while in Ventimiglia or San Remo. Less well known specialities include the local fishermen's pizza known as *sardenaira*, which incorporates anchovies, vegetables and tomato but no cheese. The region's wines are hard to obtain elsewhere and a bottle or two would make a great souvenir – look out for the light, fresh red Rossese di Dolceacqua and the fragrant white Vermentino.

No nightlife to speak of, Ventimiglia has a number of seafront cafés in which you can relax after buying your bargains at the Friday market. To experience some of the excellent pasta for which Liguria is famed, try any of the following.

Il Ritrovo dei Ciclisti e Artisti Pasta & Pizza £ This oddly named restaurant ('Cyclists' and artists' meeting place') is close to the rail station and offers good-value pasta in a vaulted ceiling basement. ⓐ Via Cavour Camillo Benso 79 ⓣ 00 39 0184 35 76 13 ⓛ Daily for lunch and dinner

Bagni Stella Marina £–££ Take your pick here between the pizzeria for light meals or more informal dining, or the ristorante for something more elaborate. In either case, you can expect friendly service and good local food and wine. ⓐ Passaggio Marconi 1 ⓣ 00 39 0184 33 89 7 ⓛ Daily for lunch and dinner

Pasta e Basta £–££ Popular with French visitors, this hotel restaurant serves imaginative pasta dishes in large portions. Booking advisable. ⓐ Hotel Sole Mare, Lungomare Marconi 22 ⓣ 00 39 0184 35 18 54 ⓛ 19.00–23.00

SAN REMO

The old name of San Remo was Matuzia, supposedly a reference to Matuta, the Roman goddess of the dawn. The town lies in an inlet between Capo Verde and Capo Nero, and is blessed with perhaps the best climate of any Riviera resort, French or Italian, hence its importance as a flower-growing centre (see page 127). It's a lively seaside resort that hosts some important festivals and has an old quarter well worth a visit. At one time it was an important commercial port under the rule of the city-state of Genoa, but the old harbour (now the Porto Vecchio) silted up and the modern port (Portosole) shelters a fishing fleet, as well as the usual cluster of luxury yachts. San Remo's seafaring tradition is embodied today in the Porto Vecchio area, which offers a pleasant half-hour stroll from Piazza Bresca along the Corso delle Nazioni as far as the 18th-century fort of Santa Tecla, which once housed the garrison of the town's Genoese rulers before becoming a prison, and now awaits redevelopment as a tourist attraction.

Pigna, the walled medieval quarter, dates back over 1,000 years and its medieval streets wind their way up the hillside to the church of the Sanctuary of Madonna della Costa and the Cathedral of San

Siro, dating from the 12th century and later rebuilt in baroque style. Just outside the old town, in Piazza Eroi Sanremesi, stands the Torre della Ciapela with its 1 m (3 ft) stone walls, once part of the town's fortifications.

Modern San Remo was discovered by the same mix of British, Russian and other European plutocrats who put Monaco and Nice on the map, and consequently exhibits some fine architecture of the late 19th century, particularly of the exuberant style known to the Italians as 'Liberty' and to the French and Anglo-Saxons as art nouveau. Like all self-respecting Riviera resorts it has a turn-of-the-century casino, built in 1905 and a very fashionable one in its day: past patrons included King Faroukh of Egypt and the Italian cinema star Vittorio de Sica, who claimed to have lost enough money there to have paid for its construction.

Fans of belle époque architecture can stroll the Corso degli Inglesi and view some beautiful examples of art nouveau and other exotic styles in the villas that line it (nearly all privately owned and not open to the public). Of particular interest is the Villa Nobel, built in a so-called Moorish style by the Swedish scientist and arms magnate, on Corso Cavalotti in eastern San Remo. It was while living here in the 1890s that Nobel decided to establish the prizes that bear his name; today it houses a Nobel museum.

This and many of the other villas possess splendid gardens that show off the range of exotic plants that will grow happily in San Remo, and many of the gardens are open to walk round. Clearly not wishing to be outdone by neighbouring Menton for the 'city of flowers' title, the municipality also provides magnificent floral displays in its public gardens, parks and flowerbeds all over town.

● *San Remo specialises in year-round floral displays*

Further evidence of the heyday of San Remo's history as a resort for wealthy foreigners can be seen in the art nouveau luxury hotels, over 20 of them that have since been turned to other uses (the town hall, for instance, was once the Hotel Bellevue), as well as the Russian Orthodox church, built on the orders of Tsarina Maria Alexandrovna in 1913.

San Remo's civic museum is housed in the 15th-century Palazzo Borea d'Olmo in Corso Matteotti: the collection is mainly of archaeological and prehistoric finds but also includes a section devoted to mementos of Garibaldi, one of the founders of modern Italy, collected by his friend Caroline Phillipson, a 19th-century British resident of San Remo. The other major cultural centre is the Rambaldi Art Gallery, with a worthy collection of Italian and Flemish masters.

Throughout the year the town hosts a full programme of events, the most important of which is the Italian Song Festival in February at the Teatro Ariston. This competition, instituted in the 1950s as a springboard for new talent, attracts not only the best of new Italian singers but also internationally known foreign artists. In the same month San Remo consolidates its position as Italy's flower capital with the International Floral Art Competition at the Villa Ormond, a must-see for garden-minded visitors.

If you're visiting in July, stay on for the International Fireworks Festival at the Porto Vecchio. Sports enthusiasts may be more interested in the San Remo Rally, a World Championship car rally in October, and the succession of internationally attended sailing regattas that take place in November and December.

Civic Museum ⓐ Corso Matteotti 143 ⓣ 00 39 0184 53 19 42
Rambaldi Gallery ⓐ Piazza San Sebastiano 17 ⓣ 00 39 0184 67 01 31

◑ *Russian Orthodox church in San Remo*

Tourist office APT Riviera dei Fiori in San Remo covers the entire coast. **ⓐ** Largo Nuvoloni 1, San Remo **ⓣ** 00 39 01845 71571 **ⓕ** 00 39 01845 07649 **ⓦ** www.rivieradeifiori.org

Villa Nobel **ⓐ** Corso Cavallotti **ⓣ** 00 39 0184 50 73 80

RETAIL THERAPY

San Remo's market is held on Tuesdays and Saturdays in the Piazza Eroi Sanremesi near the old Pigna quarter; the atmosphere is less touristy and more local than Ventimiglia's.

CAFÉS, RESTAURANTS & ENTERTAINMENT

There's a wide choice of pizzerias and restaurants in San Remo and for a break from sightseeing you'll never be far from a café in the Pigna (old town), the seafront or the Porto Vecchio/Piazza Bresca area.

San Remo Casino This is the main focus of nightlife in San Remo. In addition to gambling – mainly roulette, *chemin de fer* and slot machines – it has a lovely roof garden and incorporates an opera house, both of which stage a full programme of entertainment, and there's an excellent restaurant on site, too. Check the Casino website or with the tourist office for the current programme of events. **ⓐ** Corso degli Inglesi 18 **ⓣ** 00 39 0184 59 51 **ⓦ** www.casinosanremo.it **ⓛ** 14.30–early morning. Admission charge, and jacket and tie dress code

Graziella £ Large and friendly pizzeria in the market square outside the Pigna. **ⓐ** Piazza Eroi Sanremesi 49 **ⓣ** 00 39 0184 50 20 88 **ⓛ** Daily, lunch and dinner

ⓞ *San Remo's Porto Vecchio is a good place to take a break*

White Lady £ Efficient service and a handy location in the centre of town. ❸ Corso degli Inglesi 1 ❶ 00 39 0184 53 17 26 ❺ Wed–Mon, lunch and dinner

Plaza Café £–££ This small, centrally located trattoria is ideal for an alfresco lunch after doing the market and the sights of the Pigna. The menu is typically Ligurian, which means you'll be enjoying a new side of Italian cuisine. ❸ Piazza Eroi Sanremesi 9 ❶ 00 39 0184 57 32 97 ❺ lunch and dinner Tues–Sat

Biribissi ££–£££ If you haven't already lost all your cash in the Casino, enjoy high-class international cuisine in its highly regarded restaurant. ❸ San Remo Casino, Corso degli Inglesi 18 ❶ 00 39 0184 59 51 ❺ Daily, evenings only

Monaco has the most modern rail station on the Riviera

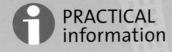

Directory

GETTING THERE

By air

Nice-Côte d'Azur Airport serves flights from many UK and Irish airlines, including Aer Lingus (from Dublin and Cork), British Airways, British Midland and bmibaby (from Birmingham and East Midlands), EasyJet (from London Gatwick, Luton and Stansted, Bristol, Liverpool, Newcastle and Belfast) and Globespan (from Edinburgh and Glasgow). Flight time from London is about two hours. Direct flights from other countries include Canada (Air Transat from Montréal, flight time 7 hrs 25 mins) and USA (Air France, Delta from New York JFK, flight time 8 hrs 40 mins).

Many people are aware that air travel emits CO_2, which contributes to climate change. You may be interested in the possibility of lessening the environmental impact of your flight through Climate Care, which offsets your CO_2 by funding environmental projects around the world. Visit ⓦ www.climatecare.org

By rail

From London Waterloo International via Eurostar to Paris (Gare du Nord) and then by TGV to Monaco can be cheaper than an airline ticket. There are five TGV trains from Paris (Gare de Lyon) to Nice – six in summer. One continues on to Monaco-Monte Carlo; the others have connections at Nice. The through train takes just over six hours, slightly more if you have to change at Nice. There is also an overnight train from Paris (Austerlitz), arriving Monaco-Monte Carlo 08.38, every night. You can avoid Paris by changing from Eurostar at Lille Europe for the train to Nice and Monaco (Mon–Fri only). The monthly *Thomas Cook European Rail Timetable* has up-to-date schedules for European international and national train services.

Eurostar reservations (UK) ☎ 08705 186 186 🌐 www.eurostar.com
Thomas Cook European Rail Timetable ☎ (UK) 01733 416477;
(USA) 1 800 322 3834) 🌐 www.thomascookpublishing.com

By road

Driving from the UK via Calais will take you two–three days to cover the
1,200km (720 miles) from Calais to Monaco: head for Aix-en-Provence
and pick up the A8 autoroute, 'La Provençale', exiting at junction 56 for
Monaco. For a more scenic approach, you can leave the motorway at
Nice and follow one of the corniche mountain roads into Monaco.

ENTRY FORMALITIES

Monaco applies the same immigration and customs regulations as
France. Since entry to Monaco is from France, there are no formalities
at the Monégasque border. You should, however, be prepared for
a random stop and search by police.

Documentation

Passports are needed by UK visitors and all others, except EU citizens
who can produce a national identity card. Visits of up to three months
do not require a visa if you are a national of the UK, Republic of Ireland,

TRAVEL INSURANCE

Monaco is not a member of the EU, and UK visitors cannot
take advantage of reciprocal health insurance. Healthcare
facilities in the Principality are excellent but expensive; all
visitors to Monaco should, therefore, carry travel insurance
which provides generous medical cover.

USA, Canada, Australia or New Zealand. Other travellers should consult the French embassy or tourist office in their own country on visa requirements, or check on the official government website **France Diplomatie** Ⓦ www.diplomatie.gouv.fr/venir/visas/index.html

Customs

Residents of the UK, Ireland and other EU countries may bring personal possessions and goods for personal use into France, including a reasonable amount of tobacco and alcohol, provided they have been bought in the EU. There are few formalities at the point of entry into France. Residents of non-EU countries, and EU residents arriving from a non-EU country, may bring in up to 400 cigarettes and 50 cigars or 50 g (2 oz) tobacco; 2 litres (two–three bottles) of wine and 1 litre (one bottle) of spirits or liqueurs. The full regulations and definitions of 'reasonable amount' may be checked at Ⓦ www.douane.gouv.fr

MONEY

The euro (€) is the official currency of Monaco, even though it is not an EU member, so there's no need to change currency when entering from France. €1 = 100 euro cents. It comes in notes of €5, €10, €20, €50, €100, €200 and €500. Coins are in denominations of €1 and €2, and 1, 2, 5, 10, 20 and 50 euro cents.

ATM machines that accept British and international debit and credit cards are not plentiful. Those at the following locations are all open 24 hours daily:

Centre Commercial de Fontvieille Ⓐ 23 av. Prince Héréditaire Albert (the main shopping centre in Fontvieille).

Crédit Foncier de Monaco Ⓐ 11 blvd Albert 1er (facing the harbour).

Crédit Mutuel ⓐ 8 rue Grimaldi (La Condamine, near the market and shopping area).

The most widely accepted credit cards are VISA and MasterCard, though other major credit cards such as American Express are also accepted in restaurants and shops. Traveller's cheques and foreign money can be cashed at most banks and bureaux de change – you may have to produce your passport or other ID. Traveller's cheques are not widely accepted by restaurants and shops. Many hotels also will change currency and cash traveller's cheques, though not always at a very favourable rate.

HEALTH, SAFETY & CRIME

Tap water is safe (if not it is marked *eau non potable,* meaning 'not for drinking') but the locals and most visitors prefer to consume one of the many brands of mineral water. Medical facilities in Monaco are of an excellent standard, but expensive – ensure you have adequate travel insurance. Most minor ailments can be taken to pharmacies, indicated by a green-cross sign. Pharmacies have expert staff who are qualified to offer medical advice and dispense a wide range of medicines. Many drugs, such as aspirin,

⬇ *Don't worry, the police are never far away in Monaco*

that are widely available in the UK are obtainable only at pharmacies in Monaco.

Monaco has one of the highest police-to-population ratios in the world, as well as video surveillance on nearly every street, and you would be very unlucky to be the victim of a crime of any kind. Although it is only common sense to keep money or valuables out of sight, both on your person and if left in a car, this is one place where you could wear your best jewellery in public (and, of course, given the average wealth of the residents, they often do). If you do encounter any trouble or lose any property, you won't have any problem locating one of the gendarmes on the street, or you can report it at the central police station, which is in La Condamine, one block away from the harbour.

Sureté Publique ⓐ 3 rue Louis Notari ⓣ 93 15 30 17 ⓛ 24 hours a day

OPENING HOURS

Shops: 09.00–12.00, 14.00–19.00 Mon–Sat
Banks: 09.00–12.00, 14.00–16.00 Mon–Fri. Banks are closed on national holidays. The exception is: **Crédit Foncier de Monaco**, near the Casino ⓛ 12.00–23.00, including Sun and holidays

TOILETS

The standard of public toilets (marked by a *Toilettes* sign) is high and they can be found all over the Principality. In addition, museums, shopping centres and cafés and restaurants have good facilities.

CHILDREN

Although Monaco is usually thought of as a playground for adults rather than children, there's plenty here to make a family holiday a success, especially as so many of the beaches of the Riviera are only a short drive away. Certainly, older children will enjoy many of

🔵 *The automata in the Musée National will fascinate kids*

Monaco's attractions – the model ships in the Maritime Museum (see page 106), the shark tank in the Oceanographic Museum (page 84), the Classic Car Exhibition (page 105), the stalactites in the

Observatory Cave (page 92), the Musée National (page 66) and even the waxworks (page 83) all have potential child appeal. And if you really want to give them a treat, you can fork out for a helicopter trip around Monaco (see page 100). For younger kiddies the Parc Princesse Antoinette (page 93) offers a supervised playground and a mini Formula 1 track, and you can safely leave your young ones to be entertained by the qualified team at one of the children's clubs at the Plage du Larvotto while you finish off your tan (see page 76).

COMMUNICATIONS
Internet
Perhaps because it is not a popular destination for backpackers, Monaco is not rich in public internet connections. However, there is an internet café at this centrally located bar/restaurant:
Stars'N'Bars ⓐ quai Antoine 1er ⓣ 93 50 95 95 ⓦ www.starsnbars.com
ⓔ info@starsnbars.com ⓛ 11.00–24.00 Mon–Thur, 11.00–02.00 Fri–Sun

Phones
The phone numbers given in this book are the local ones, which can be dialled alone for calls made within Monaco. There are no area codes. To make calls to Monaco from anywhere else in the world, dial your international access code (usually 00) followed by the international dialling code for Monaco, 377, and then the local Monaco number. Even calls from just across the border in France must start 00 377. Calls to abroad (including France) from Monaco begin 00, followed by the country code (France 33, UK 44, Republic of Ireland 353, USA and Canada 1, Australia 61, New Zealand 64, South Africa 27) and then the area code (leaving out the first 0 if there is one) and the number.

Public phones in Monaco require the use of calling cards, which can be purchased in denominations of 50 or 100 units from post offices and *tabacs* (licensed tobacconists, who also sell stamps); most public phones will also accept major credit cards, however.

Post

The central post office is in Monte Carlo, and there are others in La Condamine and Monaco-Ville. Stamps and phone cards can be bought there. Note that only Monaco stamps are valid on mail from the Principality, but they cannot be used on mail posted in France. In all other respects the efficient Monégasque postal service is integrated with the French Poste;

🔺 *A sign of true civilisation – the postboxes are red!*

postcards to the UK and Ireland will normally arrive in two–three days, taking a little longer to non-European destinations.

Current rates for sending postcards are Europe €0.50, North America €0.90, Australia and New Zealand €0.90.
Central Post Office ⓐ sq. Beaumarchais, Monte Carlo ⓣ 97 97 25 25
🕐 08.00–21.00 Mon–Fri, 08.00–12.00 Sat

ELECTRICITY

Monaco runs on 220 v with two-pin plugs. British appliances will need a simple adaptor, obtainable in the UK or at any electrical or hardware store in Monaco. US and other equipment designed for

110 v will need a transformer (*transformateur*), easily acquired locally if you can't buy one at home.

TRAVELLERS WITH DISABILITIES

Monaco's layout on a steep hillside doesn't make it the best of destinations for visitors with impaired mobility, and the buses are not adapted for wheelchairs. On the other hand, the generous provision of lifts and moving walkways around town does make sightseeing easier than it would otherwise be for visitors in wheelchairs and their companions. The period around the Grand Prix race (see page 12) is especially unsuitable, owing to the many safety barriers and fences erected in streets near the course. Many of the hotels have made provision for guests with mobility problems, as have the Classic Car Exhibition (see page 105), the Oceanographic Museum (page 84) and the Casino (page 64). The Jardin Exotique is virtually impossible for wheelchairs but most of the other parks are manageable. One car-hire company can rent Peugeot 309 cars equipped for wheelchairs: **Hertz Monaco** ⓐ 27 blvd Albert 1er, at the Ste Dévote car park ⓣ 93 50 79 60

Useful organisations for advice and information include:

Association Monégasque des Handicapés Moteurs (Monaco Association for the Mobility Disabled) has a survey of facilities for disabled people in the Principality. ⓐ 9 rue Princesse Marie de Lorraine, MC 98000 Monaco ⓣ +377 93 50 71 00

▶ *Aerial view of the city*

RADAR The principal UK forum and pressure group for people with disabilities. ⓐ 12 City Forum, 250 City Road, London EC1V 8AF ⓣ (020) 7250 3222 ⓦ www.radar.org.uk

SATH (Society for Accessible Travel & Hospitality) advises US-based travellers with disabilities. ⓐ 347 Fifth Ave, Suite 610, New York, NY 10016 ⓣ (212) 447 7284 ⓕ (212) 725 8253 ⓦ www.sath.org

TOURIST INFORMATION

The main tourist office is in the centre of Monte Carlo, at the other end of the Jardins de la Petite Afrique park from the Café de Paris. It stocks a wide range of literature and maps and has helpful staff who can make accommodation bookings and sell tickets for many attractions and events. Its website gives a very good overview of Monaco's attractions, events and practical information for visitors. There are also information kiosks in the summer (mid June–Sept) at the old rail station in La Condamine, on the quai Albert 1er at the main harbour, on the roof of the main old town car park (Parking des Pêcheurs) and in the Jardin Exotique; two other kiosks are open all year round, at the new rail station and Nice Airport.

Direction du Tourisme et des Congrès de la Principauté de Monaco ⓐ 2a blvd des Moulins, Monte Carlo, MC 98030 ⓣ 92 16 61 16 ⓕ 92 16 60 00 ⓦ www.monaco-tourisme.com or www.visitmonaco.com ⓔ dtc@monaco-tourisme.com ⓛ 09.00–19.00 Mon–Sat, 10.00–12.00 Sun

Websites

In addition to the official tourist office websites, the following sites are useful in trip planning:

Mairie de Monaco The city council's website is particularly informative on municipally administered parks, attractions and events. Ⓦ www.monaco-mairie.mc

Monte Carlo Online The English is a little quaint, but there's a lot of information on their listings search engine. Ⓦ www.monte-carlo.mc

Sites covering the entire Riviera include:
Ⓦ www.guideriviera.com (the official site of the French Riviera);
Ⓦ www.cotedazur-en-fetes.com (events on the Riviera) and
Ⓦ http://riviera.angloinfo.com (English-speaking services and information)

French Yellow Pages If you're trying to track down or contact a business of any sort, this directory also covers Monaco. Ⓦ www.pagesjaunes.fr

Listings & brochures

The Monaco tourist office publishes a range of listings and brochures to enhance your stay in Monaco, in particular *Bienvenue*, a monthly list of events combined with an at-a-glance guide to practical information of all kinds. For in-depth shopping and dining details, pick up its annual publication *Monaco Shopping*. Their little booklet *Monaco Loisirs* contains not only a city map and a bus map but also tear-out discount vouchers for just about every attraction in town that charges for admission.

Emergencies

EMERGENCY NUMBERS
Police ☎ 17
Ambulance/Fire service ☎ 18
Night pharmacy or doctor on duty ☎ 141
(if calling from a public phone ☎ 93 25 33 25 instead)
Hospital emergency ☎ 97 98 97 69

MEDICAL SERVICES
Centre Hospitalier Princesse Grace Main hospital, with 24-hour
emergency service. ⓐ av. Pasteur ☎ 97 98 99 00 (switchboard)
Riviera Medical Services English-speaking doctors on call
(not necessarily for emergencies) ☎ 00 33 4 93 26 12 70

POLICE
The Police HQ is where you should go to report or recover lost property:
Sureté Publique ⓐ 3 rue Louis Notari ☎ 93 15 30 18

EMBASSIES & CONSULATES
Addresses are in Monaco itself unless otherwise stated. The phone
numbers given are those for calling from Monaco.

Australia Embassy ⓐ 4 rue Jean Rey, Paris, France ☎ 00 33 1 40 59 33 00
Canada Hon. Consul. ⓐ 1 av. Henry Dunant ☎ 97 70 62 42
New Zealand Embassy ⓐ 7 rue Léonard da Vinci, Paris, France
☎ 00 33 1 45 01 43 43
Republic of Ireland Consulate ⓐ 5 av. des Citronniers ☎ 93 15 70 00
South Africa Hon. Consul General ⓐ 30 blvd Princesse Charlotte
☎ 93 25 24 26 ⓔ consul-afrisud@monte-carlo.mc

UK Hon. Consul. ❷ 33 blvd Princesse Charlotte ❶ 93 50 99 54
USA Consulate ❸ 7 av. Gustave V, 3rd Floor, Nice, France
❶ 00 33 4 93 88 89 55

EMERGENCY PHRASES

Help! Au secours! *Ossercoor!*
Fire! Au feu! *Oh fur!*
Stop! Stop! *Stop!*

Call an ambulance/a doctor/the police/the fire service!
Appelez une ambulance/un médecin/la police/les pompiers!
*Ahperleh ewn ahngbewlahngss/ang medesang/lah poleess/
leh pompeeyeh!*

🔺 *If you lose something, make straight for the police station*

WHAT'S IN YOUR GUIDEBOOK?

Independent authors Impartial up-to-date information from our travel experts who meticulously source local knowledge.

Experience Thomas Cook's 165 years in the travel industry and guidebook publishing enriches every word with expertise you can trust.

Travel know-how Contributions by thousands of staff around the globe, each one living and breathing travel.

Editors Travel-publishing professionals, pulling everything together to craft a perfect blend of words, pictures, maps and design.

You, the traveller We deliver a practical, no-nonsense approach to information, geared to how you really use it.